Welsh

IN WISCONSIN

Revised and Expanded Edition

Phillips G. Davies

THE WISCONSIN HISTORICAL SOCIETY PRESS

Published by the Wisconsin Historical Society Press
Publishers since 1855

© 2006 by The State Historical Society of Wisconsin

www.wisconsinhistory.org

Publication of this book was made possible in part by a gift from The Estate of Mary Williams Enerson

Photographs identified with WHi or WHS are from the Society's collections; address inquiries about such photos to the Visual Materials Archivist 816 State Street, Madison, WI 53706.

Printed in the United States of America
Text and cover designed by Jane Tenenbaum

10 09 08   2 3 4 5

Library of Congress Cataloging-in-Publication Data

Davies, Phillips G.
Welsh in Wisconsin / Phillips G. Davies. — Rev. and expanded ed.
p. cm.
Includes bibliographical references and index.
ISBN 0-87020-214-6 (pbk. : alk. paper)
1. Welsh Americans — Wisconsin — History. 2. Wisconsin — History. I. Title.
F590.W4D33 2006
977.500491'66—dc22
2006000880

⊗ The paper used in this publication meets the minimum requirements of the American National Standard for Information Sciences-Permanence of Paper for Printed Library Materials, ANSI Z39.48-1992.

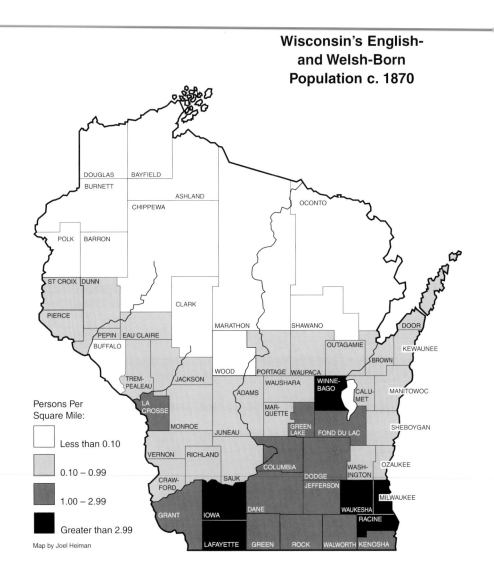

Wisconsin's English-
and Welsh-Born
Population c. 1870

Persons Per
Square Mile:

	Less than 0.10
	0.10 – 0.99
	1.00 – 2.99
	Greater than 2.99

Map by Joel Heiman

DOUGLAS BAYFIELD
BURNETT
ASHLAND
CHIPPEWA
OCONTO
POLK BARRON
ST CROIX DUNN
CLARK
PIERCE
PEPIN EAU CLAIRE
BUFFALO
MARATHON SHAWANO
DOOR
OUTAGAMIE
KEWAUNEE
BROWN
TREM-
PEALEAU
JACKSON
WOOD PORTAGE WAUPACA
WAUSHARA
WINNE-
BAGO
CALU-
MET
MANITOWOC
LA
CROSSE
ADAMS
MAR-
QUETTE
MONROE
JUNEAU
GREEN
LAKE
FOND DU LAC
SHEBOYGAN
VERNON RICHLAND
COLUMBIA
OZAUKEE
CRAW-
FORD
SAUK
DODGE
WASH-
INGTON
JEFFERSON
GRANT
IOWA
DANE
WAUKESHA
MILWAUKEE
RACINE
LAFAYETTE GREEN ROCK WALWORTH KENOSHA

RETAINING OLD-COUNTRY WAYS

The popular stereotype of the Welshman, reinforced by Richard Llewellyn's best-selling novel (1940) and subsequent film (1941) *How Green Was My Valley*, is that he was a miner who loved to sing. As with most stereotypes, there is an element of truth in this. Coal mining was an important industry in Wales, and many Welsh came to America to work in the coal fields of Pennsylvania and Ohio. Likewise, singing was and is an important national tradition in Wales, and it is difficult to imagine a Welshman who would not sing, either solo or in chorus, at the slightest provocation.

But the stereotype applies only in part to the Welsh who came to Wisconsin in substantial numbers between 1840 and 1890, for they were principally small farmers in search of arable land on which to raise their crops and their families. In this, of course, they resembled so many European immigrants who came in search of inexpensive land; but the patterns of Welsh settlement and adaptation differed somewhat from that of other ethnic groups. For example, alone among the peoples of the British Isles, they did not speak English as their native language.

Two major Welsh characteristics are sentimentality — particularly a sentimental attachment to *yr hen wlad* (the old country) — and a very extended family relationship in which even the most distant relatives are known and the exact relationship traced out in great detail. One of the most tearful moments at the annual Gymanfa Ganu reunion in Wales is the introduction of Welsh-connected visitors from overseas. The frequent use of the word *hiraeth* (translated inadequately as "longing") in Welsh-American accounts and the fact that many Welsh settlements were located in areas that were topographically rather similar to the home district attest to this sense of closeness to the homeland. Besides missing the more extensive religious opportunities in the old country, they assuredly missed the land itself — unproductive though much of it was in comparison to the American prairie. Unlike the Danes, for example, who did not cluster together and were quickly absorbed into the general populace, most of the Welsh in Wisconsin settled in close-knit communities and strove consciously to retain their religion, their national traditions, and their language. Hardworking, pious, somewhat stiff-necked, they quickly established themselves in rural enclaves (called "districts" after the old-country usage) and prospered unobtrusively, well outside the mainstream of American life.

For the Welshman, religion and language were inextricably intertwined. Although there were some English-speaking churches in Wales in the nineteenth century, most were Welsh-speaking. Three churches — the Baptists, the Wesleyan Methodists, and the Congregationalists — had links with the English-speaking denominations, but the Calvinistic Methodists were an exclusively Welsh church. Most of the Welsh immigrants who came to Wisconsin were members of the latter two denominations. Since the church was a major center for community activities and because the Welsh language (often called Cymraeg) was regularly spoken there, the language was still being used with considerable frequency in churches and in newspapers and magazines of the Wisconsin Welsh as late as the 1920s and 1930s. The persistence of their language, and the bonds supplied by a strongly church-oriented society, produced a group of immigrants whose descendants, even today, retain a sense of themselves as a special ethnic group. But their numbers were so small, and they clustered together so clannishly in rural hamlets, that they made no really substantial imprint upon the face of Wisconsin.

The Welsh came to Wisconsin quite early. Although the state is now noted for its German, Polish, and Scandinavian immigrants, the Welsh were comparatively numerous at one time. In fact, there were more Welsh, Scots, and English in Milwaukee than Germans in the early 1850s, though by the 1860 census there were about two-thirds more Germans than British-born residents. (One problem in dealing with Welsh immigration figures is that some data, such as that above, lump the Welsh together with the English and the Scots. This is particularly unfortunate in that it has led to the supposition that the Welsh spoke English. In fact, during the mid-nineteenth century, the lower classes in Wales — meaning those who tended to emigrate — spoke about as much English as the average American visitor to Paris speaks French.)

In contrast to the present, when the use of Cymraeg is declining there, Wales was predominantly (70 percent) Welsh-speaking in 1870. One of the earliest Welshmen to encourage immigration to America, and who himself knew little or no English when he came to this country in 1821, emphasized this point when he wrote in 1841: "In going to America there are many difficulties to overcome — leaving one's native land, traveling over the sea, learning a new language, new customs — in a word, to go to America, is a revolution in a man's life."

COMING TO WISCONSIN

Possibly the best overview of the extent of Welsh immigration to Wisconsin can be found in the federal census figures for 1900, despite the fact that the Welsh had begun to arrive as early as the 1840s. For Wisconsin, that census lists 3,356 people born in Wales and 7,866 Welsh children born in America — a total of 11,222. Pennsylvania, Ohio, New York, and Illinois had a larger number. There were two urban centers — Milwaukee (1,606) and Racine (1,124) — although many Welsh in the latter were probably farmers in the rural areas of Pike Grove and Skunk Grove (now known as Franksville), where two of the earliest Welsh churches in the state were established. The major rural settlements were in the counties of Columbia (1,365), Waukesha (1,060), Iowa (972), and Winnebago (806). Smaller Welsh settlements were and still are to be found in Sauk, Jefferson, Rock, and La Crosse Counties.

The Reverend Robert D. Thomas, a Welsh-born American clergyman, writing in 1872 and basing his conclusions on visits to most of these settlements a few years earlier, concluded that, in addition to the smaller enclaves mentioned above, there were 18,260 Welsh in the larger settlements, divided approximately as follows:

Milwaukee	1,000	Waukesha	3,000
Racine	2,500	Iowa	2,885
Columbia	5,000	Winnebago	1,400

Thomas, an ardent advocate of Welsh immigration to this country, may have overstated his case, but his approximations are probably more accurate than the census figures because the latter listed only those born in Wales and their children. By 1870 there would have been second- and third-generation children as well as youths who had come from the eastern states to Wisconsin and would not have appeared in the federal statistics. It is also possible that by 1900 the Welsh population in the state had declined somewhat because of westward migration. Accounts of many other Welsh settlements, particularly in Minnesota, South Dakota, and Washington, frequently refer to a number of former Wisconsin residents. The settlement at Lime Springs, Iowa, for example, was almost exclusively made up of Wisconsin people in its early days.

The use of the word *settlements* may raise some question. Unlike the Danish immigrants, who were advised not to settle close to each other and to learn English as quickly as possible, the Welsh dreamed of a Welsh state, or at least of exclusively Welsh communities. As described by the Reverend Michael D. Jones, who hoped to establish such a community in this country in the 1840s, such a state would embrace "The free farmer on his own property, and on his hearth the song of the harp and the company of the Welsh language. . . . There shall be there a chapel and school and a meeting house, and the old tongue as the means of worship and business, learning and government."

In fact, caused by their desire to continue to use the Welsh language and to remain in their Welsh-speaking churches, most Welsh wished to separate themselves from other nationalities and to maintain their differences even from the other peoples of the British Isles. Not only did they frequently show prejudice against the British, which had often been the nationality of the oppressive landlords from whom they had fled when leaving Wales; but in early accounts, they occasionally spoke disparagingly of the "Americans," who shared a common language with their former oppressors, to say nothing of the whiskey-drinking Catholic Irish as well as the beer-guzzling, Sabbath-breaking Germans and Scandinavians. As a result, the Welsh avoided, particularly in the nineteenth century, intermarrying with other national groups. They tended to settle near each other, to worship in their own churches, and to cling to their language, their customs, and their religion.

Many of the early Welsh settlers in America, the Welsh Friends or Quakers particularly, were fleeing from religious persecution. Others, primarily seeking economic advantages, were farmers who settled in New York, Pennsylvania, and Ohio. Settlers began to flock to the iron and coal districts of Pennsylvania in the 1830s. Nationwide, these early Welsh settlers were about evenly divided between the agricultural and the industrial and mining groups.

The first known Welsh in Wisconsin seem to have been John Hughes and his family of seven, who came to Genesee in Waukesha County in 1840. By 1842 there were fifteen families and ninety-nine Welsh people in the community, which is now a part of a rural area surrounding the town of Wales. Many Welsh chapels were constructed in this district — the most famous being Capel Log (The Log Chapel), originally built in 1845, the oldest Welsh Presbyterian church west of the Great Lakes. The cemetery associated with it, like the city cemetery in Dodgeville, contains an extremely large number of monuments for the Welsh settlers, quite a few of them with inscriptions in Cymraeg.

Welsh migration to the agricultural districts appears to have come to a virtual standstill by 1890. Immigration patterns are confused by the fact that while some came directly from Wales to Wisconsin, there was also a constant westward drift of Welsh (mostly farmers) from New York to Pennsylvania, from Pennsylvania to Ohio, from there to Illinois or Wisconsin, and from there to Iowa, Minnesota, Nebraska, South Dakota, Colorado, Washington, and Oregon. This movement was caused not so much by the Daniel Boone spirit as by the lure of available land. As Welsh-American farm children in the East reached their majority, land in the home district had become difficult or expensive to buy; thus they were forced to move westward.

LEAVING WALES

The reasons why the Welsh first came to America, and more specifically to Wisconsin, were partly the same and partly different from the reasons that motivated other immigrant groups. Wales was a small and mountainous land. Farm land was scarce, and the farmers there were either tenants on land owned by English-speaking Anglican or Welsh landlords, or Welsh farmers who had very small holdings of their own. The Welsh language was discouraged by the educational system, and the more wealthy were forced to pay taxes to support the Church of England, to which few of them belonged. The allure of the vast New World was obvious to the poor, hemmed-in Welsh yeoman. In an attempt to indicate the size of America, one advocate of immigration in 1866 said that Lake Michigan was "large enough to bury three countries the size of Wales underneath it." Another, somewhat earlier, estimated, "If one were to divide all the land, good and bad, between all the inhabitants of Wales, there would be only 4½ acres of land for each person!" In America, of course, 160 acres could be had for next to nothing. In general, then, the availability of inexpensive or essentially free land in large quantities under American preemption laws (1841), and later the homestead laws (1862), enticed the Welsh to the Midwest. The former law allowed the purchase of 160 acres of land at $1.25 per acre and a modest registration fee (in Wisconsin the fee was $18).

J. R. Daniel, one of the first settlers at Proscairon (Green Lake County), was eloquent in his old age on the subject of hunger for land: "A question asked of me many times was: what advantage was there in settling in a place so new and disadvantageous. Our answer was, cheapness of land." He stated that many from the old neighborhood had come across the sea encouraged by the local reports of inexpensive and productive land and the existence of an already established Welsh community.

In 1856 the Reverend Robert D. Thomas, the Welsh-born Congregational minister who tirelessly promoted immigration to America and later wrote a massive history of the Welsh in America, presented a forceful summary of conditions in Wales and reasons for immigration. After praising the beauty of the land in Wales, he stressed that there was essentially no available land in the principality: "It is unbeneficial to cry, 'Very good land' and 'The best land under the heavens' when there is no way to possess it nor to enjoy it, and to be able to put one's foot on it."

Nor had farming any future there. Thomas inveighed against the hard-hearted landowners and overseers who "unmercifully despoiled" the Welsh tenant farmers. Wales was controlled by large landowners who rented out portions of their land to tenant farmers. Only a very small number of farmers owned their land. (Although the widespread practice of primogeniture has at times been blamed for the bleak conditions in the Welsh countryside, the individual holdings were usually so small that it could have had little effect.) By the post-Napoleonic period, however, conditions worsened because the Corn Laws not only made the import of cheap food from abroad impossible but also tended to force up the price of food at home. As the historian Edward G. Hartmann has written, many Welsh farmers were close to starvation: "Discouraged at their lot in the homeland, encouraged by glowing accounts of the great opportunities awaiting them in the new nation, many became brave enough to cut the ties with their loved ones, to risk the dreaded ocean voyage, and to chance their lot in the new world." Thus, conditions in Wales were ripe to encourage immigration to America.

To a large degree it was the nonconformist clergy — the most respected group in Wales — who most encouraged it. Although some opposed it as overly materialistic, several wrote books and pamphlets about opportunities in the United States in which the availability of farmland was stressed much more than factory or mining work. In addition, other books as well as letters sent back home, many of which were published in newspapers and magazines in Wales, were influential in attracting more Welsh newcomers to America.

These books and pamphlets published in the mid-nineteenth century discouraged the lazy, the drinker, and the elderly from coming to America but strongly urged "sober, industrious, and faithful" young people to take advantage of their opportunities. They also consistently remarked on the relatively high prices in the eastern United States, where one might have to pay from twenty to fifty dollars for an acre of land even if vacant land was available, and pointed out that it was much less costly in the western states. Of Wisconsin, one Welshman said that it "has much of the richest land in the Union, and its reputation is high as an excellent land in which to raise wheat of all sorts as well as other grains. It has much land which is even and wavy, much like the surface of the sea. It is not so low and flat as to be wet, nor is it so hilly as to hinder agriculture. Also, it has enough wood on it to satisfy needs of all kinds." "Wisconsin Territory is the place for the Welsh," wrote John H. Evans to a countryman in 1842. "This lies to the north of Illinois and it is said that the country is extremely healthy, the water clean, the air pure, and the climate temperate."

One of the earliest such letters from Wisconsin, published in Wales in 1844, catches the enthusiasm of a land-hungry Welshman, Thomas Evans of Dodgeville (Iowa County), for what he found in the state: "Wisconsin is superior to all the states and the Canadas. It is a healthy country with wonderful water, prairie, and plenty of farm land. . . . There is no work to be done cutting down large trees and the land costs five shillings an acre. One can have it for a year without paying through preemption rights and many have lived on farms here for four years without paying a penny."

THE JOURNEY TO AMERICA

What then of the process of getting from Wales to America in the 1840s? The newly arrived Cheshire brothers, John and Isaac, who came to Racine in 1846, cheerfully reported: "we were eating our last piece of ham about one hour before landing at New York. We had about six or seven pounds of butter left and a good deal of flour and oatmeal bread . . . " They make the whole experience sound rather like a picnic. But only the relative cheapness of the trip seems enticing in other reports. Many immigration advocates, for instance, insisted on extreme caution both in Liverpool (the port from which most of the Welsh sailed at this time) and at Castle Garden (a common port of entry) in New York. Don't trust strangers, stay in Welsh hotels, beware of drinking, they advised.

That the transatlantic voyage itself could be a nightmare was attested to by the Reverend Jenkin Jenkins, who preached at Welsh Prairie (Columbia County) in the 1850s. In 1841 it took him three months to make the journey. "We had very stormy weather, and we were blown out of the Bay of Biscay and the Azore Islands; yes, we were nearly taken to Bermuda, and then back until we were in sight of New London. For eight days we were living on one biscuit a day along with a little water. Seven were buried at sea, and one may well imagine that we had a pretty bad look to us by the time we got to New York."

The pious, self-contained Welsh immigrants observed with disdain the antics of their Irish shipmates: "During the whole journey when the sea was quiet there was nothing to be heard except their singing, dancing, shouting, and noise. I saw them at it shouting, playing cards, playing the flute, dancing, etc., even on Sunday. . . . But on the first stirring of the sea they were like snails pulling in their horns and running to pray in a minute."

Precise prices for sea travel are somewhat hard to determine. Sailing ships and steamships were both in use during this time; there were several classes of accommodations; prices varied widely from line to line and even from passage to passage. Still, fairly accurate approximations can be made. The sailing ships crossed from Liverpool to New York in twenty days to six weeks with steerage costing between three and five British pounds and cabins at between fifteen and twenty-five pounds. Steamships took from ten to fifteen days, and third class cost eight pounds, eight shillings, or about $33. (The pound equalled about four American dollars, the shilling about twenty cents.)

Food was provided in all classes, but travelers were strongly urged to take some of their own: "It would be useful to you . . . to have a little good cheese, oat cakes, boiled ham, onions, lemons, apples, etc. so that you and your wife and children will be able to have a little food . . . between the times of the regular meals on the ship." Aboard the steamships, there was usually enough good food, including bread that was baked every morning. A day's meals were arranged about as follows:

> *At eight in the morning.* — Coffee, sugar, and fresh bread and butter; or cold bread with butter; or oat flour, porridge, and treacle. *At one o'clock.* — Beef or pork and broth soup or soup with bread and potatoes, or fish and potatoes according to the day of the week. And on Sunday there is pudding. *At six o'clock.* — Tea, sugar, cold bread and butter. Two quarts of water are given to every passenger every day.

Not all Welsh immigrants fared so well on shipboard, however. John Owen wrote in 1867: "There were many unpleasant things but the food was the worst. We had breakfast at eight o'clock, comprising tea and coffee every other day, a warm loaf with a little butter but that little was too much for me; its smell was enough, let alone its taste. At one o'clock two men came round with a jug of stew as if they were distributing it to pigs." Another Welshman wrote of dinnertime on the transatlantic passage: "It is the nearest thing in the world to feeding time at Wombwell's animal show." The "half-filling, stinking codfish" was particularly despised, and some Welsh stoically fasted on Fridays rather than eat it.

The route that the Cheshire brothers took was typical for most of the immigrants to Wisconsin at the time. Having landed in New York in the spring of 1846, they took a steamboat to Albany and the railroad to Buffalo ($5.50 per person). From there they took a boat through the Great Lakes to Racine. Those who came from the eastern states either took the railroad or a combination of Ohio River boat and railroad. The New York and Erie Railroad's fee from New York to Racine was reported by Thomas in 1854 as being one pound, thirteen shillings, four pence (about $6.65). In 1872 he said that the charge was about three cents a mile.

Although both of the Cheshire brothers took jobs in Racine — Isaac at a store, where he later reported that he was learning accounting and making $60 a year, and John as an apprentice at a saddler's shop — the majority of the Wisconsin settlers became farmers as soon as possible. On the other hand, it was frequently necessary for the new immigrants to earn some money in the cities of the East or on the coast of Lake Michigan before they moved farther west. For instance, one of the earliest settlers at Proscairon, Thomas H. Roberts, worked in a brick yard in Racine for some time before he moved to the country. Advocates of immigration, however, firmly suggested that as little time as possible be spent in the large cities because of their manifold temptations for a foreigner.

URBAN LIFE

Racine, the earliest Welsh urban settlement in Wisconsin, was ambiguously both urban and rural. Calvinistic Methodist and Congregational churches had both been established there in 1843. The congregation of the former numbered 194 members. Each denomination also had a rural church, the former at Skunk Grove four miles west, with twenty-seven members, and the latter at Pike Grove, three miles north, with a "strong and faithful" congregation, many of them from Montgomeryshire and Merionethshire. (There also were Welsh in the lead and zinc mines of Iowa County in the early days, but apparently such settlers were not numerous, did not stay long, and have left little trace.)

Precise details about the occupations and way of life of the urban Welsh are difficult to find, but contemporary publications mention influential Welsh businessmen in both Milwaukee and Racine. In the former, "there were over a thousand Welsh . . . many of whom are starting to speak English rather than Welsh. There are some very rich Welshmen. The 'Lake Brewery' was once owned by Mr. Owens, but it now belongs to Powell and Pritchard." Strangely enough, it was this Welshman, Richard Griffith Owens, who established Milwaukee's first brewery in June 1840. He and his two partners improvised a five-barrel brew kettle serviced by a tangle of homemade pipes, tubes, and auxiliary barrels; by July they were supplying barley-based Milwaukee Brewery Ale to thirsty local patrons. (Not *all* Welshmen, obviously, regarded alcohol as the Devil's drink.) Owens, a native of Anglesey in Wales, and his sons later operated the Atlantic Hotel. As to Milwaukee churches, the Calvinistic Methodist chapel on Michigan Street had eighty members and a congregation of two hundred; the Congregationalists on Jefferson Street had a chapel with fifty members and 150 in attendance as well as a branch church south of the center of the city, in the Bay View area.

Near the turn of the century a Welsh-American visitor to Racine found a Welshman who owned a hotel, various Welsh "capitalists," artisans, and two lawyers. Several years earlier, in 1889, he had remarked, "It is likely that the Welsh element is more evident and honorable in proportion at Racine, than it is in any other town in the States." In 1843 nearly 10 percent of Racine's population was Welsh. Later there was an exclusively Welsh volunteer fire engine company and two Welsh-born mayors.

RURAL LIFE AND AGRICULTURE

In the early days, Welsh immigrant farmers followed one of two main patterns: buying an already established farm, or homesteading. The relatively wealthy, such as Richard and Margaret Pugh of Waukesha County, bought already established farms. In 1846 they wrote back to Wales that they had "bought an improved farm with house, buildings and eighteen acres of wheat ready sown. The whole farm consists of 160 acres well fenced." They had bought two yoke of oxen, four cows, six yearlings, pigs and sheep, and various types of poultry four miles west of Prairieville (the old name for Waukesha) near other Welsh settlers.

Another letter of 1847 published in Wales told of the availability of other improved farms: "Within five miles of Racine there was a farm of 120 acres with a house and buildings on it and with about twenty-five acres already cultivated for $800," and of "a very good farm with a house and new buildings on it, eighty acres in size with about half of it cultivated, within four miles of this town and with a chapel and a school nearby, price $1300."

In contrast to most of the Welsh who took pains to settle near one another, a few, such as John and Margred Owen of Baraboo (Sauk County), did not. Although generally pleased with conditions in 1848, they sorely missed their countrymen: "We have as neighbors three

Frenchmen, one Dutchman, four Irishmen, one Yankee, and from fifteen to thirty Indians, so that we have had no religious meetings but family meetings from September until now, but better times are coming. Two Welsh families are coming near us and we hope soon to have public worship."

Things were much more primitive in the Proscairon settlement. An old settler, Hugh H. Morris, described the traditional American way of building a log cabin: the announcement of what he called a "raising," when "a large group of neighbors would come there to raise it, so that before night the walls had been raised and the owner could finish it himself." Obviously "the day of the raising was a great day for the family where it was held."

Even more primitive were the so-called sod huts in which many of the early settlers lived, which were merely "a cellar which had been dug out of the earth with logs across the top and bushes over that; and finally earth was put over it all as a top." This was commonly the lot of the less-well-off Welsh in the wilder territory west of Racine. Few of the Welsh came with furniture; their beds and chairs had to be made by hand. Because of space limitations, the small beds used by the children had to be tucked away under the large beds during the day. Chairs were little more than stools, three or four feet high. Often a clothes chest was used as a table in cramped quarters.

Before factory-made cloth became readily available, the women of the household had to make nearly all of the clothes for the family — stockings, gloves, blankets, and underclothing as well as outer garments. Fortunately the Welsh immigrants, with their background of extensive sheep farming and working with wool, were able to put their old-country abilities to good use on the frontier. Of women's clothing, one Welsh woman remarked, "The manner of dressing was simple. A calico dress was considered to be respectable enough at that time, and good enough to use under all circumstances. Nor would anyone ever think of not going to religious services if she did not have a hat or bonnet nor anyway to get one. A hood made at home would serve rather than neglecting to attend the services."

The food that the Welsh ate was essentially that of England: simple meat, often in the form of stew — mutton was their favorite — and potatoes, usually boiled. They tended to prefer oats to other grains and were very slow in coming to accept corn (stigmatized as "Indian corn" in the early days). Oatmeal was a staple at breakfast, and various kinds of oat cakes, baked on a bake stone or iron griddle, were eaten throughout the day. *Bara brith* ("speckled bread," resembling unsweetened fruit cake) was the most popular of their ethnic dishes and is still served regularly at meetings and celebrations and to visitors. Tea was preferred to coffee, and honey to sugar; both cheese and butter were widely used. Since it was customary to do no cooking on the Sabbath in the old days, the Welshman's Sunday meal was served cold or else had been prepared the day before.

Farming methods were primitive in the Wisconsin wilderness. An old settler at Proscairon described planting corn: "Two people would put holes in the furrow with an ax, and two would follow along and put the grain in them and tread the hole closed. They went at a walk and frequently at a run, and the task was accomplished excellently. The next thing was to thresh the winter wheat and to gather a small amount of it with the old harrow and the toothed wood, and fail to keep the chaff; but all in all, we got a more excellent crop than we had ever seen in the Clwyd valley [in Wales]." Many early settlers told stories of the intractable oxen that they used for clearing land and plowing; most also complained about the condition of the roads and the long distances from farm to market. Hugh Morris of Proscairon recalled, "At first they were forced to go from twenty to forty miles to get flour, and it took several days for the trip with oxen. The nearest grain markets for years were Milwaukee — eighty-five miles, and Stevens Point; the market for meat and flour was nearly the same distance." The first minister to be ordained by the Calvinistic Methodists of Wisconsin was forced in 1848 to travel over a hundred miles from Proscairon to Racine "with a team of oxen hauling a load of wheat, which he marketed on the way. Rain fell as he crossed the marshes on the logways. The wagon became mired and he had to carry the load of grain, sack by sack, to firmer ground where the oxen could pull it, and then reload. When he reached Racine, the future foremost preacher of the gymanfa was tired and bedraggled. But after some rest and a clean-up he preached three times."

THE RELIGIOUS COMMUNITY

There was a saying among the Welsh in America: "The first thing a Frenchman does in a new country is to build a trading post, an American builds a city, a German builds a beer hall, and a Welshman builds a church." Churches were indeed central to the Welsh way of life. Except for the Quaker, Mormon, and Anglican groups to which some Welsh belonged, but who are without relevance to early Wisconsin, most of the Welsh in Wales belonged to one of four denominations: the Calvinistic Methodists, the Congregationalists, the Baptists, and the Wesleyan Methodists. In America they were members of the same churches, except in the cities where some joined the English-speaking "American" churches.

Some Welsh had no specific religious ties, although particularly in rural areas they often attended services and supported the church even though they were not formal members. (This accounts for the large disparity between figures for church members and "attenders.") Also relevant is the fact that among these denominations people did not become church members at the time of baptism but in young adulthood or in later life when they would be examined upon their beliefs. Membership was not automatically granted.

In 1872 Reverend Thomas estimated Welsh-speaking church membership in Wisconsin. There were a total of eighty-three churches — most of them with chapels — slightly over half of them Calvinistic Methodist. There were forty-six Welsh-speaking ministers and fifteen preachers. Membership totaled 3,695, and attenders numbered nearly three times as many, 9,180.

The Calvinistic Methodists (*Trefnyddion Calfinaidd*, or T.C.), with slightly over 2,300 members out of the total of 3,695, were the most powerful group in the state, although nationwide the Congregationalists were equally strong. Calvinistic Methodism — an amalgam of Calvinist theology, Methodist religious fervor, rejection of control by bishops, and strong self-government through synods and presbyteries — had a national and statewide district organization that was heavily structured compared to the looser organization of the Welsh Congregationalists. Like all the other Welsh denominations, the T.C. opposed the use of alcohol, was more mildly opposed to tobacco — particularly in the early days — and strongly believed that the Sabbath should not be desecrated by secular activities. Only its insistence on the use of the Welsh language in its religious services kept the Calvinistic Methodists from uniting with the northern branch of the American Presbyterian Church. Such a merger finally took place in 1919. The Wisconsin Calvinistic Methodists Gymanfa became the Welsh Wisconsin synod of the Presbyterian church. It was transformed in 1934 to become the Welsh Presbytery of Wisconsin. Twenty years later, in 1954, it disbanded and the member churches joined their area presbyteries.

The Welsh Congregationalists (*Annibynwyr,* meaning Independents in Welsh) differed primarily because of their insistence on the autonomy of the individual church; but the group seems to have had no serious doctrinal differences with the Calvinistic Methodists.

Slowly, over a period of time, the Congregational churches abandoned the Welsh language and/or amalgamated with English-speaking congregations and, lacking a strong central leadership, faded imperceptibly into the American religious scene. The Wisconsin Congregational Gymanfa came to an end in 1916. But as long as they used Cymraeg in their services, they were separate churches that could make little intimate contact with the English speakers in the community.

Ideologically similar, save for their insistence upon baptism by immersion, were the Welsh Baptists. Never as strong as the Calvinistic Methodists or the Congregationalists in America, they were relatively strong in Wisconsin, having eleven of their national total of seventy-one churches there. The Wisconsin Baptist Welsh Gymanfa was organized in 1860 and dissolved about thirty years later. The Wesleyans, for the most part English-speaking Welsh, were not a strong group in Wisconsin or elsewhere in America and never had their own association.

Most is known about the Calvinistic Methodists because after the national denomination merged with the Presbyterians, a valuable history of the group was published; and because of the group's great strength in Wisconsin, the book contains considerable material about the state. In summary the book remarks, "The Wisconsin Gymanfa had a rapid growth. Within twenty-five years from its inception it consisted of nearly fifty churches. At its zenith it was the largest gymanva in the Welsh General Assembly in America." At one time it consisted of six presbyteries and extended over a large area that for a time included Illinois, Iowa, and Kansas.

All of these Welsh churches were governed by twice yearly Gymanfas to which most of the ministers, deacons, and interested lay people came. Although the schedule varied somewhat, it usually included a Tuesday afternoon business meeting and sermons in the evening. On Wednesday morning from 8 to 11 the ministers and deacons met to discuss business; in the afternoon there were ordinations, and more sermons were given in the evening. On Thursday there were more meetings from 8 to 10, sermons at 10 and 2, and at 6 there was singing, reading, and praying. At times as many as seventeen ministers, most of them local but some from other parts of the country or from Wales, took part. Each preacher usually gave several sermons during the meetings. Welsh congregations were noted for their attentiveness and their willingness to dispute a clergyman who strayed from the text; it was commonly said that the Welsh, unlike the English, *knew their Bible.*

RELIGIOUS EDUCATION
AND SOCIAL LIFE

Before the church building — or more properly, chapel — came the Sunday School, which was basically a Welsh development. Not only did it teach religion, but it had also been the main means of teaching reading and writing to the Welsh lower classes in the old country. Typically, almost immediately after a few Welsh arrived at Proscairon, a school was established in a private home. On the first Sunday of November 1844, some of the new settlers met. John J. Evans, who later became a minister, is said to have remarked to two other Welshmen: "Boys, I'm almost broken-hearted to-day; my thoughts, for hours, have been in the old Cefn-y-Waen Church [in Wales] . . . and I have come down here to this wilderness." He then took his Bible and walked to an old shed in the woods. "The two men followed him, joining him in reading verses in turn and questioning each other after the manner of a Welsh adult class. Before leaving they resolved to invite all the Welsh in the vicinity to meet the following Sunday at the home of Mrs. Catherine Foulkes, where the first Sunday School was organized."

The construction of the earliest chapels was a community affair: "Every family, if it was able, would prepare one or two pieces of wood and bring them to the appointed place." Then work would begin. The first chapel in the Columbus area measured only about 24 by 18 feet, "the door on one side of it and the pulpit at the other end, with windows on the other sides of it and two other windows on each side." Unfortunately, few such rural chapels remain in Wisconsin. Peniel, built in 1856, and Bethesda, built in 1848 or 1849 and rebuilt in 1856, both in Winnebago County, are two survivors. In Picatonica (now commonly spelled Pecatonica) district in Iowa County there is Peniel, built in 1850 (outside of which can be found a monument to its long-time minister, the Reverend John Davies); and Carmel, built in 1854 and rebuilt in 1885. Salem or Rock Hill in Green Lake County was organized in 1846. The latter is "the lone survival of the old-style Welsh church in Wisconsin . . . built of bricks and almost square. . . . The seats are graduated, like seats in a gallery, row of seats one step above the one in front . . . two aisles divide the seats into these sections. Each pew has a door, which swings on hinges and is fastened with a clasp. Between the pews and the pulpit stands the stove." As in New England Puritan churches, men and women sat on opposite sides of the chapel. Most of the chapels were quite small and usually were constructed of wood, particularly in the countryside. Reed organs were used as soon as it was possible to purchase them, although a piano was and still is used in addition to the organ to accompany congregational singing.

Most Welsh social life also revolved around the churches. There were the Sunday Schools for children and adults, and singing practice, for the Welsh prided themselves on their part singing, which was aided in the nineteenth century by the development of the "Sol-fa" system of musical notation, allowing people to sing in parts without any formal knowledge of musical theory. Fortunate was the district when the Gymanfa or Presbytery, with its two- or three-day festival of sermons, came to the neighborhood. There were also periodic revivals, when many of the attenders and occasionally outsiders saw the error of their ways. A contemporary account tells that "at the end of a warm and effective meeting on Friday night . . . the old tender hymn, 'Come, My Holy Jesus With Your Mortal Wound,' was sung eloquently in Welsh with the last part repeated again and again, and having had the spirit descend upon them, they broke out in happy praise. Several of the old experienced saints were compelled to give way to their feelings." As a Welsh minister later said, "Good singing produces an atmosphere. It arouses our deepest emotions.

It makes members of the congregation receptive and the task of the preacher easier."

It was customary among the Welsh to hold prayer meetings, usually on Wednesday evening, in private homes. In them, many men who eventually became preachers or ministers had their first experience in leading religious meetings. Particularly in the 1870s, temperance meetings also enjoyed something of a vogue. Although deadly serious to the Welsh, they were not entirely without touches of humor. When one such meeting in the late 1840s was in the planning stage at Proscairon, a man objected, reasonably enough, since it was then quite impossible for anyone in the area to find anything alcoholic to drink.

His view did not prevail, however, because of the minister's sharp analogy: ". . . Nothing has done more to destroy the Welsh nation than the trade in liquor . . . and it is best that we prepare ahead of time to resist it. It would be a pale hope for the safety of the great cities on the shores of the sea if they waited without preparations until the navy of the enemy attacked them. They have fortresses and cannons and guns and have learned to use them already. We ought to prepare in the same way for this enemy." (Although most of the Welsh were, in truth, total abstainers, there were exceptions. Occasionally hollow trees and barn lofts could be found containing large numbers of bottles that provided mute evidence of solitary drinking!)

Among the most secular activities were Fourth of July celebrations, which were held in most of the districts. At daybreak the Welsh of the area would gather together and go to the prescribed meeting place in carriages. A description of one such meeting at Proscairon in 1849 tells that "Before them waved the temperance banner, and on it was a picture of a kingly eagle with its wings expanded in freedom and joy." There were several addresses, some in English and some in Welsh, on such subjects as "Freedom"; and hymns and anthems, including the Hallelujah Chorus, were sung. America's independence day was not drowned in beer or hard cider, as elsewhere.

And, of course, among the Welsh, there was always singing. The Cheshire brothers found no lack of it in Racine. They asserted that "there is better singing here by far than ever was in Carneddau or Llangollen either. One of the greatest singers that Caernarvonshire ever possessed lives here." They claimed to have heard some of the most "magnificent anthems which Handel wrote, the greatest composer of the world, one of which is called the Hallelujah Chorus, 'Lift up your hearts,' etc. You asked whether our religious breathren were English or Welsh: Welsh. There are about five hundred Welshmen living in this town." Before the demise of the Welsh-language churches in the early twentieth century, the singing was mostly restricted to the churches and to Fourth of July celebrations. Later the Cymanfaoedd Ganu (singing assemblies) became very popular.

Another Welsh tradition was the Eisteddfod (literally, "a sitting"). Although probably of very ancient origin, it was revived in Wales in the nineteenth century. This type of meeting of poets, musicians, and literary persons was held in various places and with various degrees of importance both in Wales and America. The most impressive ever held in this country was the four-day Eisteddfod at the World's Columbian Exposition in Chicago in 1893. People from Wisconsin took prominent parts in it, though it was truly an international event with some choirs, singers, and contestants coming all the way from Wales. The Eisteddfod choir, made up mostly of people from Milwaukee and Racine, was directed by John H. Williams and E. O. Jones of the two towns, respectively. The Reverend Fred Evans also conducted singing, and many other Wisconsin Welsh took part, including Miss Jennie Owen of Milwaukee, who sang at several of the programs.

Local Eisteddfodau (the Welsh plural form) were held in Wisconsin just as they were in various places in the Midwest and East, most frequently on or near January 1, July 4, or St. David's Day (March 1; named after the patron saint of Wales). Wherever they were held they included competitions in singing, poetry and prose writing, oratory, and the like. Even children took part in the local ones, and money prizes were offered. Cymraeg was used almost exclusively until the early twentieth century, when English took over and even non-Welsh competitors were permitted to take part.

Courtesy Margaret Walters

Evan and Dave Walters on the John Hughes homestead, Springwater Township, Waushara County

WHi (X3) 38706 (Courtesy Mrs. Leonard Knebel)

The Edward Jones farm in the Pecatonica Welsh settlement, southwestern Iowa County

Courtesy Mrs. E. H. Roberts

Gathering stone for Edward Roberts's silo, near Randolph, Columbia County

WHi (X3) 38795 (Courtesy Margaret Walters)

Potato harvesters taking a break on the David Lloyd Jones farm, Waushara County, 1918.

WHi (X3) 38792 (Courtesy Lee Morgan)

The Joseph Davies family of Wild Rose harvesting potatoes assisted by hired diggers, 1911.

(Courtesy Mrs. Leonard Knebel)

Lead miners in the Peacock Mine near Rewey, Iowa County

WHi (X3) 39055 (Courtesy Martha J. Jones)

Robert K. Jones's hardware store, Wild Rose, ca. 1910

WHi (X3) 38846

Elizabeth Davies, Vira Davies, Laura Miller, Jennie Miller, and Eunice Miller preparing food in the Peniel Church at a Gymanfa Ganu (Welsh songfest) near Pickett, Winnebago County, 1946.

WHi (X3)38711

Carmel Church, Welsh Presbyterian, in Mifflin Township, Iowa County

WHi (X3) 38707

Peniel Church, Mifflin Township, Iowa County, picturing the Reverend Griffith Griffiths, his family, and members of the congregation.

WHi (X3) 38843

John Williams leading Welsh singers at a Gymanfa Ganu in the Penial Church near Pickett, Winnebago County, 1946.

WHi (X3) 38790 (Courtesy Lee Morgan)

The Morgan quartet, ca. 1900, a group of Welsh singers who performed throughout Wisconsin

Right: Gymanfa Ganu at the Peniel Church near Pickett, Winnebago County, 1946

Below: Gymanfa at a church in Randolph, Columbia County, 1912

WHi (X3) 38839

Courtesy Mrs. E. H. Roberts

WHi (X3) 38842

A moment of repose during a Gymanfa at the Penial Church near Pickett, 1946

WHi (X3) 38791 (Courtesy Lee Morgan)

Tyddyn Llwyn Derw (Oak Grove Farm) near Pickett, Winnebago County, ca. 1910

LIVING   FAITHFULLY THROUGHOUT THE WEEK

Despite these joyful occasions, Welsh life in Wisconsin was a fairly austere life because of the primitive conditions, the serious Calvinistic religious orientation, and the lack of what now passes for amusement. Yet one finds signs of a strange tenderness among the people in some contemporary sources. David Jones Davies, who once lived in Proscairon, apparently shocked his fellow farmers in Minnesota by advocating coexistence with, rather than extermination of, the gophers. A contemporary recalled: "When the little gophers began to destroy the corn, and all had a plan of destroying them completely, he asserted that they had no right to do that, for they were the small creatures of the great Creator, and that it would be more reasonable to save them and feed them by scattering the corn along the surface of the land amply enough so that there would be no need for the little things to be forced to destroy the crop." And William D. Davies, reporting on a visit to Wisconsin in 1889, approached sentimentality in his concern for the horses of the parishioners. He said that after a recent religious revival, the people decided to make a shed in the shade of the chapel for the horses, adding: "Although the Bible teaches that it is godly to care for the food and comfort of the animals, I am surprised that so many rural churches compel their horses to remain outside in the exceptional weather for hours, summer and winter, while they themselves are in the chapel."

Along with their interest in singing, both choral and solo, the Welsh had a fascination for public speaking and especially for debate. During the 1850s in Columbus, for example, heated formal discussions took place on such subjects as "Who had done the most good for the world, the farmer, the businessman, or the artisan?" "Was Moses or Paul the greater man?" and "Is the married or the single life the best?" In fact, the Welsh loved meetings both inside and outside the church. There were cultural and literary meetings, usually centered upon competitions in poetry writing and singing, Eisteddfodau, and meetings of the Bible and the temperance societies.

Most of the Wisconsin Welsh were farmers. Although it would be interesting if they had differed in important ways from their American neighbors and those of other ethnic backgrounds, there is little evidence that they differed materially in what they raised or how they raised it from other immigrant peoples of northern Europe. Their farms were mainly grain-producing, and most early reports naturally emphasized wheat production. In the area near Oshkosh, for instance, several varieties of wheat were tried until it became apparent that corn and soybeans were better suited to the land. At first livestock were kept primarily for the use of the family rather than for sale or dairy products. Later, the Welsh were pioneers in cheese production, and all their settlements had at least one cheese factory. Early Welsh settlers frequently established a sawmill if waterpower was available in the area. Taken all in all, the Welsh farmer was known for his hard work and frugality.

The Welsh valued education highly. Their attempt to preserve the Welsh tongue in no way discouraged attendance at the English-language schools when they became available. Before that time, however, schools were often held in the chapels, with reading from the Bible and prayers before actual studies began. The local minister was frequently also the schoolmaster in these early days. Most of the sons of the immigrants later attended Carroll College in Waukesha, sponsored as it was by the English-speaking Congregational church. In the mid-nineteenth century, though, many a young boy could attend school only in the winter because his labor was needed on the family farm. Many of early schools were open only during the winter when little farm work could be done.

In sum, then, the Reverend J. A. Jones's comments when he visited the Proscairon district in 1856 seem to have been true rather than merely complimentary: "The people lived their life faithfully throughout the week — no drunkenness, murdering, breaking the Sabbath, swearing or cursing. The men were hard working in the fields and the wives kept their houses clean and warm, and a hearty welcome was given to strangers by every family throughout the neighborhood. They were excellent American citizens and strong Prohibitionists to the core."

Because of their strong opposition to slavery and the liquor business, Jones could well have added *and Republicans* between *strong* and *to the core*. The Welsh strongly supported Abraham Lincoln and the Civil War. A Welshman living in Bristol (Kenosha County) wrote his brother in the old country that prior to the war, "Four million people were under the oppression of slavery. A law was in force compelling every white man to be a hunter of the black and . . . the great Mississippi River was blocked by troublemakers and murderers and many other awful things were giving the country a terrible appearance." In Wisconsin, as in surrounding states, the Welsh joined the Union Army in large numbers. In the Winnebago settlement, fifty-two Welshmen enlisted; ten of them died, one of them at Andersonville prison in Georgia. Seventeen veterans of the conflict are buried in the Cambria cemetery. William Rowlands of Welsh Prairie wrote in 1863: "Eighteen [men] were wanted from this district and they were all found, volunteers all, except that we gave $100 bounty to each and most of these were Welsh. Many places failed to meet the demand and the result was drafting."

British support of the Confederacy reawakened old anti-British sentiment among many of the Welsh. One settler in Rosendale (Fond du Lac County) went so far as to blame the assassination of Lincoln on the British: "there are many leaders [of the conspiracy] still at large, fugitives from their country, hiding under Queen Victoria's petticoats; but the sign of Cain is on them while they live." At war's end, two people from the Columbus settlement — the Reverend Thomas E. Hughes and Elizabeth M. Evans — with the support of their community, did missionary work among the Southern blacks.

Some Welsh settlers also became involved in another important event of the time, the California Gold Rush. Though there may have been others, the records show that eight men left Proscairon in 1852. Two of them died on the journey, one of whom was "buried on the south side of the road near Thousand Springs," in northeastern Nevada. Two others died in California.

UNITY IN A NEW LAND

Just as it had been the clergy who were responsible for bringing many Welsh to Wisconsin, so were they the most respected members of the communities and at times the subject of a biography and selection of sermons after their deaths. Although most clergymen were very mobile, a few remained in the same district for an extremely long period of time. Among these we find such Calvinistic Methodist clergy as John Davies of Pecatonica (Iowa County), born in Wales around the year 1814. He came to Pecatonica in 1847, was ordained three years later, and served the Peniel and Bethesda churches until his death in 1877. He became the subject of a biography written by a fellow minister. Thomas Foulkes was born in Wales in 1818, and, after a brief time in New York, he was ordained in Wisconsin in 1849 and spent the rest of his long life in Welsh churches in Racine (Winnebago County) and in Randolph (Dodge County). He died in 1892, and his son carried on in the ministry. Another, John J. Roberts, was born in Wales in 1819 and came to Wisconsin in 1845. After preaching in the Columbus district he was ordained and remained there until his death in 1890.

More commonly, however, a minister would not stay in a church for very long, partly because being a clergyman among the Welsh in the early days was not a full-time job. Most of them and their families could not have lived on the scant remuneration provided by the small groups they served. (Salaries were to a great extent given in the form of local produce in these early days.) Thus, in the agricultural districts, most clergymen owned farms or did manual labor like everyone else, and in the cities they carried on some sort of trade or profession in order to survive.

Yet it is noteworthy that clergy from Wales continued to be attracted to the Welsh settlements of America throughout the nineteenth century, a condition that tended to keep the language alive and to consolidate ties with the homeland. But despite their desire to keep their original language and churches, the Welsh were encouraged by the advocates of immigration and their ministers to become American citizens as soon as possible. Reverend Thomas advised in 1854: "Every EMIGRANT ought to get his citizenship within five years after landing in America, but he must be careful to give two years' warning about his intention to become a citizen in writing to the national court." His charge was widely followed, for few of the Welsh intended to return to their native land. Census figures for 1900 and 1920 confirm that the Welsh were the immigrant group with the highest proportion of fully naturalized citizens.

Still another unifying factor in the lives of the Welsh emigrants was the mass of writing, published in America, in the ancient language of Wales. Essentially secular, and containing news both of Wales and of the Welsh settlements in North America, was *Y Drych*, (The Mirror) founded in New York City in 1851 but published in Utica during most of its life. *Y Drych*, in its earlier days, soon swallowed up several similar publications. It appeared as a weekly until 1940 and moved its offices to Milwaukee in 1960. Until the 1930s it was almost exclusively written in Welsh, although English-language advertisements became rather common during World War I and later. By the 1950s only some of the obituaries and very little else were in Welsh. It is now published in St. Paul, Minnesota, and continues its original editorial policies, though almost none of the paper is in Cymraeg.

Every issue contained at least one or two detailed reports from Wisconsin written by local representatives. During the early twentieth century the pages of *Y Drych* included a wide variety of materials. Besides accounts of affairs in various Welsh communities there were poems, sermons, some news from Wales, including obituaries, birth, marriage, death, and ordination notices, references to the departure and arrival of ministers from their churches, and local Eisteddfodau — in general, anything that would keep Welsh-Americans aware of happenings both in the old country and in other Welsh enclaves in North America. Non-Welsh-oriented news was almost completely restricted to a large picture of the incumbent president and vice president after each national election. (Thus Welsh papers were different from most foreign-language newspapers, which lay much more stress on events in the old country and in America in general and often attempted to inculcate patriotic feelings for America by recounting famous events in American history and explaining American customs.)

Without doubt, the newspaper provided a strong bond between the numerous settlements of the very mobile Welsh throughout the country even well into the twentieth century and tended to preserve a sense of separateness among the people. At one time the circulation of *Y Drych* was as high as 12,000. Indicative of a strong recent revival of Welsh ethnic consciousness was the introduction of another monthly newspaper, *Y Ninnau* (Us, or We Also) in 1975. Based in New Jersey and including considerably more articles along with language lessons in Cymraeg, it quickly gained a relatively large circulation.

Three major religious monthlies were also published in Welsh. They, like *Y Drych*, had apparently large circulations as long as the Welsh churches survived. One, *Y Cyfaill* (The Friend) (1838 to 1933), was sponsored by the Calvinistic Methodists and later by the Presbyterian Church. Another, *Y Cenhadwr* (The Missionary), associated with the Congregationalists, was published from 1840 to 1901. The Baptists, always the smallest group, sponsored *Y Wawr* (The Dawn) from 1876 to 1896. Much like *Y Drych*, all three magazines contained birth, marriage, and death notices, church news, sermons, essays, and poetry. Many other newspapers and magazines were published for the Welsh-Americans; a Sunday

School journal, *Y Lamp* (The Lamp), published in Oshkosh from 1897 to 1903, was representative. In addition, books, most of them theological works and biographies of famous Welsh-American ministers, were published — most frequently by T. J. Griffiths in Utica — until the turn of the century.

Nevertheless, church services conducted in Welsh slowly disappeared after the turn of the century. In general they ceased first in the cities (in Racine in 1905), though they continued in rural areas (Peniel in Winnebago County and Carmel in Iowa County until 1921 and in Cambria as late as 1944).

SOCIAL AND CULTURAL LIFE

The Welsh in Wisconsin were relatively few, and not every little settlement was fortunate to have its history written or its earliest settlers captured within the covers of a typical "commemorative and biographical record," paid for by subscription, in the last quarter of the nineteenth century. But enough is known about some enclaves to infer a good deal about the social and cultural life of the Welsh settlers as a whole. For example, a detailed book about the Waukesha County settlements, written in English in 1926, includes material about most of the families who settled in the county, together with information about churches, clergy, schools, literature, music, and (inevitably) "prominent citizens." The author estimates that the Welsh population in the county was, at its height, about 1,200 people, 95 percent of them living in a circular area of four and a half miles centering on the relatively newly established town of Wales at the junction of present highways 41 and 83. At the time of this writing, Jerusalem Church, the successor of Capel Long, in Wales, still had an active congregation descended from the original one founded there in 1842; and Bethesda Church had an active congregation in the Kettle Moraine Parish. The Welsh spirit lives on in this area.

Next to Milwaukee and Racine, Columbus (in eastern Columbia County) was the largest city in the state to have a large number of Welsh both in the countryside and the city. A book about the Calvinistic Methodist churches in the area points up one fairly major fact about the Welsh settlements, namely that the churches tended to be small —

seldom more than seventy-five members — either because of the desire for democratic self-government or the fact that doctrinal contentions often caused part of a church to establish its own organization elsewhere in the community. In Columbus, however, there seem to have been no such contentions. When a church became larger, a daughter church was established. (In the early days, of course, the difficulties of traveling tended to spawn small churches as well.)

Six Welsh people arrived in Columbus in the summer of 1845 and immediately started a Sunday School. There were fifty-five church members by the end of the year, and at one time as many as thirty-five new settlers lived in one of the few houses in the area. Most of these came from North Wales (Caernarvonshire and Anglesey in particular), although several resettled from New York. By 1848 there were 205 Welsh settlers, eighty-five of them church members of the various denominations.

The first Bethel chapel was built in 1846. By 1850, when there were one hundred church members, the chapel was rebuilt and decorated with a clock bearing the inscription: "Bethesda Chapel. What can this be except it be the house of the Lord. Built in 1850."

Another rural chapel, Salem, slightly to the east, was constructed in 1848 and rebuilt in 1857. In the next year a chapel was built in the town itself because several Welsh businesses had been established there. Finally, in 1878 Moriah Chapel was built. As an example of Welsh mystical piety, a local legend about its precise location is noteworthy: "As Wm R. Hughes and his wife one night were passing by a glade, they thought that they heard pleasant singing just above their heads. The old Mrs. Hughes, in her own simple way, said, 'You know what, Will, there will be a chapel in this place sometime, wait and see.' Whatever explanation can be given for this event today, this old couple looked on it as a very significant thing." None of these rural chapels survives.

Many of the Welsh farms in Wisconsin, according to the custom in Wales, were given names — usually the name of the farm or the district from which the family had emigrated. Because of the sparsity of Welsh surnames, these designations were useful in distinguishing among the several John Joneses or David Williamses in the settlement. Among the farm names near Columbus were Pen y Daith (End of the Journey), Bryn Mawr (Big Hill), Ty Hen (Old House), Y Plas (The Manor), Ty'n-y-Coed (House in the Wood), and such place names as Hendref and Bryn Hafod.

Occupational nicknames were also probably used here as they were in most Welsh districts. Thus at Proscairon one finds reference to John Owens the Church (presumably because he was a deacon) and John Owens the Singer.

The fiftieth anniversary of the beginning of the Welsh settlement in Winnebago County was marked by a two-day celebration at Bethesda Church in 1897. The Welsh first moved there from Waukesha County in 1847, and by the early 1850s there were sixty-four families. But by the next decade the number had dropped to forty-two — much of the loss caused by a large migration to a new settlement in Clay County, Iowa. As in Columbus, there were four Calvinistic Methodist chapels, but in addition the Congregationalists had three and the Baptists and Wesleyans one chapel each. Of them, however, the Calvinistic Methodists were the strongest, both in Oshkosh (Salem Church was founded before 1873) with 103 members and in the rural area at Bethesda with sixty-five members at the time of the celebration in 1897.

The Welsh Prairie district in Columbia and neighboring Green Lake County is quite spread out. Today its chief market town is Randolph, but for years it had centered on Cambria (a poetic synonym for Wales).

The Calvinistic Methodists were strong there. At their height, the district (in this case including Columbus) had twenty-one chapels, 1,305 members, and 1,663 in the Sunday Schools. The Reverend Rees Evans claimed in 1894, possibly erroneously, that it had been the center of Welsh America at the time: "If a preacher comes from the Old Country, he has not been in America if he has not been in Wisconsin, and he has not been in Wisconsin if he has not [been] in Cambria and the districts here."

In the early days, Cambria was the hub of the area. One contemporary account described it in general terms: "There are many hundreds of respected Welsh living there. They include farmers, merchants, and craftsmen. This is a healthful and pleasant place, and it lies between the populous Welsh districts of Welsh Prairie and Portage. These Welsh came here early enough that they got their land free or for low prices, and they have done well. The emigrant, after coming to these parts, will feel as if he were in the land of this birth as far as religious observances are concerned."

But the Reverend Robert D. Thomas correctly prophesied that the town would not grow very much. In 1857, he said, "Cambria was a small,

beautiful town then, having just been built up. . . . At that time I thought
that Cambria would become a populous and successful town; but, to my
amazement, when I visited in September 1870 it had grown very little."
He blamed this condition on the fact that the Welsh "neglect to pay
proper attention to the need to build towns and to establish businesses
in them in order for their settlements to succeed." Here, as elsewhere, the
Welsh preferred the farm — even a small one — to the city. Cambria
still contains an active First Presbyterian church that has many Welsh
associations.

Although there are no records for the Dodgeville area in Iowa
County that are comparable to those for the settlements of Welsh Prairie,
the story of this once quite populous Welsh settlement can be pieced together. With Dodgeville as its hub, the district included primarily rural
areas northeast of the town: The Wood, Jenneton, and to a degree the
villages of Blue Mounds (which is in Dane County), Ridgeway, Barne-
veld, and Spring Green far to the north and just across the county line.

In 1845 a Welsh Calvinistic Methodist chapel was built slightly west
of Dodgeville at a place called Welsh Hollow. The town church was built
in 1849 and rebuilt in 1882. Most of the other chapels in the area were
built in the 1850s, and many continued to exist until the turn of the century. The group at Bethel, north of Blue Mounds, however, came to an
end in 1885 when most of the farmers left for Minnesota.

In the extreme southwestern part of Iowa County was the Picatonica (now Pecatonica) district. In 1980 a history of Rewey, the largest town
in the area, was published, containing considerable material about the
Welsh settlement there, which was begun in 1846 by emigrants from
Pennsylvania. Although some Welsh were associated in territorial days
with the zinc mines in the district, and from the very start with small
businesses in the villages, most were typically farmers who started with
forty-acre holdings and gradually became the almost exclusive holders
of a seven-by-ten-square-mile area. Despite early-day troubles with
cholera and smallpox, the settlement flourished and four churches were
established, one by each of the three main denominations. The fourth,
Carmel, was the result of John J. Jones's desire to wield more power
in the Peniel church than the majority of the congregation wished to
grant him.

Perhaps the most unusual resident of the Picatonica district was,
strangely enough, a black man known as James D. Williams. Born a slave,

he came north after the Civil War and lived for twenty-eight years with the John H. Williams family. Not only did he adopt the family's surname, but he even joined a Welsh church, sang hymns in Cymraeg, and jokingly claimed to be "the only Welsh Negro in history." After forty years in the community working at odd jobs, he died in 1903. His gravestone still stands in Carmel cemetery.

Robert D. Thomas visited and described twenty-four districts in his book *Hanes Cymry America* in 1872. About some, such as Bangor, Fish Creek, and Blaen-y-Dyffryn (all in La Crosse County), Wild Rose in Waushara County, and Berlin in Green Lake County, very little is known, although a Welsh-background church still exists at Wild Rose.

Late in the nineteenth century, William D. Davies visited many of Wisconsin's Welsh districts at a particularly interesting juncture; it was about this time that Wisconsin had its largest Welsh population. This was also just before the demise of the specifically Welsh churches and the sharp decline in the use of Cymraeg. Davies first visited the state in 1882 in search of funds to repair the Hyde Park Calvinistic Methodist Church in Scranton, Pennsylvania, whose foundations had been undermined by neighboring coal operations. He seems to have been at all of that denomination's churches as well as several others, collecting a total of $935.98 — more than he had received in any state except Ohio — and he praised Wisconsin's thirty-two churches for their generosity to the missionary society. In 1870 the Wisconsin Calvinistic Methodist churches had 2,692 members who contributed an average of $1.18 to the work. (By comparison, the New York, Pennsylvania, and Ohio members contributed less than twenty-five cents per capita.)

Davies later became the traveling representative for *Y Drych* and paid visits to Wisconsin in 1883–1884, 1886, and 1891. He was particularly pleased to see how well the temperance movement was progressing. He thought that "about half of the Welsh in the settlements already were full prohibitionists," and asserted, "If the people throughout the land are as excited in relation to this point as they are in the Welsh districts of Wisconsin, there must be more force in the movement than many are aware of." During his 1891 visit he saw a thousand people at a Welsh-sponsored temperance meeting in Sparta. But as the nineteenth century drew to a close, many Welshmen had already moved farther westward, and Davies noted that Wild Rose was "one of the most deserted regions to my view that I have ever seen on all my travels."

CONCLUSION

What then can be said in summary of the 140-year history of the Welsh in Wisconsin? Except for Frank Lloyd Wright — the grandson of Welsh pioneers who settled at Spring Green and whose famous home, Taliesin, was named after a Welsh poet — none of them or their children achieved national fame. After a careful survey, Edward G. Hartmann was able to name only seven other "Distinguished Welsh-Americans" from Wisconsin. Three of those were judges: John T. Jones (d. 1891) of Iowa County; Evan Alfred Evans (d. 1948) of the United States Circuit Court; and David Evan Roberts (d. 1918) of Douglas County. The other four were an English professor at the University of Wisconsin, Edward Thomas Owen (d. 1931); Harriet Davies (d. 1952), an Oshkosh physician and medical missionary in India; John Pugh Davies (d. 1908), a Racine steel industrialist; and the Reverend Jenkin Lloyd Jones (d. 1918), a Unitarian churchman and militant pacifist. One might also add to the list Llewelyn Breese of the Proscairon district, who was Wisconsin Secretary of State in 1869 and a strong supporter of Welsh immigration. But this is a small showing for this proud and self-conscious people.

For the most part, in truth, the Welsh element in Wisconsin has consisted primarily of farmers, small-town businessmen, and craftsmen. Few are known outside their immediate locales, and many of these Welsh-Americans still consider themselves separate to a degree from the larger communities in which they live. Their accomplishments have been modest, but some of them have gone to considerable effort to document their history and preserve their traditions. Those who are proud of their Welshness subscribe to Welsh-American newspapers, and long before genealogy became a national pastime, many Welsh were fervently doing research about their ancestors. The relatively affluent visit Wales occasionally; the less so seem contented to save their money in order to attend the National Gymanfa Ganu, which has been held around Labor Day every year since 1929. (It was in Milwaukee in 1951, 1958, 1970, and 1997; Gwynn J. Parri of that city was its president in 1975–1976.) At it some two thousand people of Welsh heritage come together for both small and large group singing of hymns, to listen to professional musicians from Wales and elsewhere, and in general to associate for several days with people of similar backgrounds and interests.

On the local level, the Wisconsin State Gymanfa Ganu is held in one of the Welsh churches every year, and there are long-established Cymanfaoedd at Rock Hill (Green Lake County), Peniel (Winnebago County), and Cambria (Columbia County). In 1978 a Christmas gymanfa was begun in Columbia County. The larger cities — Milwaukee, Oshkosh, Racine, and Waukesha — still had St. David's Societies as late as 1969, and today there remains a Welsh women's club in Milwaukee. But in Wisconsin, at least, the singing assemblies seem to be the primary transmitters of Welshness to the newer generations. It is here, too, that the Welsh language is the most alive. One or two of the verses of many of the hymns are sung in Cymraeg, and someone usually leads the congregation in the Lord's Prayer in Welsh. Although most of the attendants can no longer read the language or speak more than a few phrases, being able to *sing* the words in the old tongue is considered a necessity.

The Welsh remain conservative in politics (antiabortion literature and keep-prayer-in-the-schools petitions are sometimes circulated at Cymanfaoedd), and they continue to be opponents of liquor and to a lesser degree of tobacco. Although they have lost many of their specifically Welsh churches, several — almost all of them directly descended from originally Welsh-language ones — still remain in Wisconsin. Elsewhere, Welsh-Americans are a strong force in the Presbyterian and Congregational churches to which most of them now belong.

Thus, though far inferior in numbers to many other ethnic groups that settled here, the relatively few thousand who left their homes in mountainous Wales have made their mark upon the Wisconsin landscape in little towns such as Wales and Cambria and in the Welsh inscriptions in many a small cemetery. They have kept their native language and their churches alive for nearly a century, and many of their descendants still prosper here. The sound of hymns sung in Cymraeg may still be heard in their few remaining chapels.

Photo by John Nondorf

Left: Pride in their Welsh heritage remains strong among citizens of the Village of Wales, 2005.

Above: Jerusalem Presbyterian Church, one of the nation's oldest continuing Welsh American congregations, rests at the corner of Main and Park streets in the Village of Wales.

Photo by John Nondorf

Photo by John Nondorf

Jerusalem Presbyterian Church in Wales

Y
BIBL CYSSEGR-LAN,

SEF

YR HEN DESTAMENT

A'R

NEWYDD.

Yr holl Ysgrythyr sydd wedi ei rhoddi gan Ysprydoliaeth Duw, ac sydd fuddiol i athrawiaethu, i argyhoeddi, i geryddu, i hyfforddi mewn cyfiawnder:

Fel y byddo dyn Duw yn berffaith, wedi ei berffeithio i bob gweith-red dda. 2 Tim. iii. 16, 17.

RHYDYCHEN:

ARGRAPHEDIG YN ARGRAPHDY Y BRIFYSGOL,

TROS Y FIBL GYMDEITHAS FRYTANAIDD A THRAMOR,

A sefydlwyd yn Llundain yn y Flwyddyn 1804;

QUEEN VICTORIA STREET, BLACKFRIARS, LLUNDAIN.

SM. PICA 8vo. GYDÂ Chyfeir.   M.DCCC.LXXXII.   CUM PRIVILEGIO.

Rhydychen [i.e., Oxford] : Tros y Fibl Gymdeithas Frytanaidd a Thramor, 1882.

Cofiant y Parch. John Davies, Picatonica, Wis. Gan y Parch. William Hughes.

Above: John Davies was a Calvinistic Methodist clergyman, born in Wales, who went to Pecatonica in 1847 and served churches in the area until his death in 1877.

Left: Title page of a late nineteenth-century Welsh Bible

Below: Parade float of the Caersalem Church, Wild Rose, Waushara County, 1903. On their way to the Sunday School picnic are a great many young Joneses, Evanses, and others of Welsh extraction.

WHi (X3) 38838

Gymanfa Ganu at Peniel Church near Pickett, 1946

WHi (X3) 38841

Attendees of the 1946 Gymanfa Ganu at Peniel Church near Pickett relax and engage in a lively discussion.

Hanes Cymry America by Robert D. Thomas (Utica, New York: T.J. Griffiths, 1873).

The Liverpool and Great Western Steam Company published this ad in Robert David Thomas's book *Hanes Cymry America*, a history of the Welsh in America.

James D. Williams, born a slave in Virginia, moved to Iowa County after the Civil War and adopted many Welsh customs. He jokingly called himself "the only Welsh Negro in history."

WHi (X3) 38709

WHi (X3) 38713

Gruno Mine, Mifflin, Iowa County

WHi (X3) 38786

Moses Morgan, Welsh farmer, in his garden, pre-1920

WHi (X3) 38798 (Courtesy Margaret Walters)

Members of the Davies and Thomas families pose with their horses at James E. Davies homestead near Wild Rose, Waushara County, ca. 1900–1901.

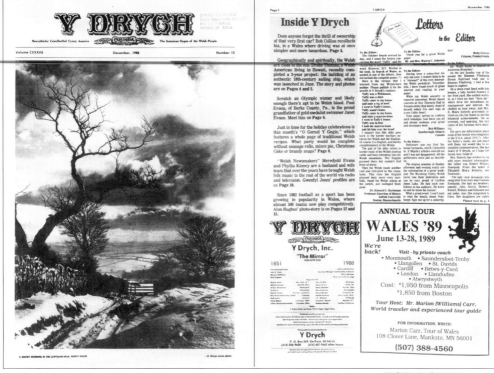

Cover and masthead of *Y Drych*, "The Mirror," a Welsh American newspaper established in 1851, published for a time in Milwaukee, and now published in a merged publication with *Ninnau*, another Welsh American paper.

Morgan and Jones family gathering in the late 1920s near Pickett, Winnebago County

Acclaimed architect and Welsh American Frank Lloyd Wright pondering a project with his apprentice, W. Wesley Peters.

WHi (X3) 46782

ph mss 842 12R

The exterior of Taliesin, Frank Lloyd Wright's home in Spring Green. Taliesin is a Welsh word meaning "shining brow," so named by Wright because he situated Taliesin on the brow of a hill.

OWEN FAMILY LETTERS, 1847–1907

The following letters are among the Owen Family Letters, 1847–1863 and 1907–1912, in the Wisconsin Historical Society Archives. The collection comprises photocopies of original letters, most of which are in Cymraeg, and transcribed translations thereof done in the late 1950s by Griffith Milwyn Griffiths of the National Library of Wales, which holds the original letters.

The letters here span sixty years and fall into two distinct groups. Earlier letters describe the trials and risks of coming to a new land and provide a good description of central Wisconsin at mid-nineteenth century. Later letters detail attempts by Owen family descendants to recover their Welsh traditions after sixty years of assimilation had eroded their Welsh identity.

The first letter is signed by John and Margred Owen, who wrote it from their new home in Baraboo (Sauk County), Wisconsin, to family members in Vaner, Near Dolgelley, Merionethshire, North Wales. John and Margred were among the early Welsh immigrants to Wisconsin, leaving Llanelltyd, Wales, in 1845 or 1846 and stopping for a time in Ohio before moving on to settle in Baraboo, in the summer of 1846.

The translation was edited by Wilbur S. Shepperson and originally published in the 1959–1960 winter issue of the Wisconsin Magazine of History.

Baraboo, Near Fort Winnebago, Wisconsin
May 27, 1847
Mr. Griffith Owen, Vaner [variously
spelled Vanner and Faner] Near Dolgelley,
Merioneth Shire, North Wales, Old Britain

Dear brother & Lowri & little Griffith:

I hope you will be in good health when you receive these few lines, as we are at present. I am sorry I have not written to you before; it is due to my negligence. It gives us great pleasure to receive a letter from you, although I am afraid that my long silence encourages you not to write. If you spare a shilling to post a letter to me every month, we shall be very pleased to have it. Tell everyone who inquires after us that we think the country will prove very agreeable to us. We are only sorry that we did not come earlier; but "better late than never."

The land in general is exceptionally good, and although thousands come here the country is so immense that there is yet plenty of government land. There are miles of it near me not yet taken. Many have come here since I came, but we were the first Welsh family to cross the Wisconsin River. It is difficult to obtain government land without paying a higher price for it than the government price. The natives are grasping, claiming the land before the Welsh. The Welsh settle before they go far enough into the interior to find government land, the price of which is 5s. 3d. of your money.

I do not know where to begin giving my news. I do not know what Will [William] said in his previous letter. I will try to answer the question you asked. I found Mr. Griffith Richards, of Dolgau a very kind friend; he spent several days with me, in his gig, showing the country. He bought a wagon for 8 pounds, oxen at 4 pounds a head and cows at 2 pounds 10 shillings a head. By the time I had bought glass, nails, a saw, and shears to build a house, and after acquiring government land and food in readiness for our arrival here, I had but one pound left, but Providence took care of us excellently. Will and Owen found work; we earned eight pounds and in that way got food for winter. From that you can see that we only had just enough to come here. We have very good land, it is as level as Dol Sauson there in Faner, if it is not too low lying. We may have a square mile of it if we have success and health to pay for it when we recover from the fever. Deio and I sawed pine trees at the end of the winter and the beginning of the spring, and we exchanged them for flour, pork, sugar, and tea. We have had plenty of food after all, and the flour comes to the house in barrels continually.

We were rather depressed at times. I was shaking with fear that the Lord was unwilling that we should come here, but your last letter completely ended the debate in our minds; the mighty hand of Providence has looked after us exceedingly well, everywhere. Although we have no reserves of money, if we have good health for a few years we shall be able to pay you and everyone else everything. Will has earned from fifteen to twenty pounds this spring; he has not come home yet, we expect him every day. I shall have that money to buy cattle. I shall receive from ten to twelve pounds from William [Bebb], Margred's brother; he has turned out a very good man. I mean therefore to buy some cattle; if I go down the river a little way I can get cattle at £2 or £2.5s. a head. This is a good place for selling butter; the butter at Faner was quite yellow at the beginning of the summer, but the butter here is much more yellow. The price of corn and flour will rise here presently. A barrel of flour now costs

£1.5s. of your money, and the potatoes are 2s. [per bushel]. This is the best place I have ever seen for men to obtain work, and sufficient money to support their family well. Good men earn from 4s. to 8s. of your money [per day].

As the country is so new, we are rather mixed; we have as neighbours 3 Frenchmen, 1 Dutchman, 4 Irishmen, 1 Yankee, and from 15 to 30 Indians; therefore, we have been without means of grace except in the family from September until now, but better things are dawning. Two Welsh families are coming near us and we hope to have public worship soon. One whole family is religious, and the wife in the other. Tell the children at Llanelltyd School to make the most of the Sunday school and of the gospel. It is the only principal thing; thousands in America despise it, but it is the only thing we have a longing for — that is our old friends with whom we worshipped. Remember us all kindly to them, especially the members of the society. You are our friends still, although we may never see each other again. I hope you will continue to remember us at "the throne of grace."

The necessity for missionaries is as great here as on the Kassia Hills and in Brittany and other places, and there is need for men here of whom the ungodly will be afraid. No Welsh is preached nearer than a distance of eighteen miles. There are thousands around us perishing for want of spiritual guidance. Between whites and Indians this country is ready for the great harvest. That is, they are ready for the Gospel. There are more Welsh Methodists than anything else in Wisconsin. There are ten preachers here, but the churches are so young and so weak that it is as yet impossible to accomplish much. Remember Wisconsin in America the first Monday night of the month. [Welsh Methodist missionary prayer meetings were commonly held on Monday night.]

Remember me to Owen and Chati [Catherine] and try to get John and Lewis Jones to give £100 to bring them here. There is plenty of land here, and plenty of tobacco at a very low price, and tea at 1s. 6d. to 3s. a pound. And remember me to [name torn from letter] Williams and Lewis Williams and everyone who remembers me. Send me a letter as soon as you can with news of yourself. How does Mr. Jones the steward behave toward you and Mr. Williams of Tyddyn [a farmstead]? You have £14 or £15 to recover from that account if you are to obtain justice. Tell [name illegible] that we are perfectly satisfied now and are at peace since we have come here. All the children and ourselves send her our regards, and

Peggy implores her to tell Lowri often to be an honest girl towards her uncle and to be sober and to fear the Lord. "Favour is deceitful, beauty is vain, but a woman that feareth the Lord, she shall be praised." Tell Evan Roberts of Cwmynack and Owen Williams of Arthgalt that I intend to write to them quite soon and give them as much news of the country as I can.

It was hot here during this summer, and they say drier than it has been for years. The corn [small grain] in most places was beginning when we came to Wisconsin, and within three or four weeks it was ripe enough for cutting. The harvests follow each other immediately. Much hay is cut after the corn is carried in. Some have an engine which threshes the corn in the field and leaves the straw behind in the fields. It started freezing a little about November, and began snowing at the beginning of January. We had a very hard frost until about the middle of March, and from two to three feet of snow. It thawed gradually with no storm as in the old country; the heat of the day thawed it. Spring is late here this year. A large amount of winter wheat is frozen; parts of Wisconsin and Illinois have failed completely. Much of the Indian corn has failed, having been planted too early; and so perhaps America may learn something about scarcity and high prices.

I am,

John and Margred Owen

The following letter, from William G. Bebb to "uncle," was probably sent to the old country from Van Wert County, Ohio. There were two William Bebbs among the Owen family clan records. The first to arrive in America was a rising politician in the 1830s and 1840s. He was elected governor of Ohio in 1846, the year he sponsored the migration of a group of about sixty Welsh persons, led by his cousin, another William Bebb, most likely the author of the following two letters.

[Undated, circa 1850]

Dear Uncle,

I am availing myself of this opportunity of writing to you. You admonished me many times to write to you often, but somehow it is easier to promise than to fulfil. I have often thought of writing to you but postponed it each time. We as a family have been in very good health since we left Wales, especially so, considering the distance we have traveled and the change of climate endured, and all things considered we have now settled down quite well. The Welsh people in the neighborhood have enjoyed fairly good health this year; the indispositions most frequently met with are the ague and the remitting [intermittent] fever. The climate here is slightly warmer in summer than it is there and colder in the winter. We had very little rain from April until the beginning of this month, but we have had a little frost some nights. The roads are the worst feature of this part of the country; the land is generally good, but much of it has not yet been settled. My mother has enjoyed good health throughout, except that she had a touch of ague last October; at times too she yearns for the religious meetings of Wales. My mother sends her fondest and kindest regards to you and Uncle Owen, and likewise to Auntie Afowin, and my uncle at Sgubor, and Auntie Bryndu and Pegi Sion. Lowry and Dafydd unite in sending their regards to you and Uncle Owen and little Owen and especially Griffith; I should very much like to see him. Tell him I would gladly pay the postage of a letter from him if he had the time to write one. Griffith, give our regards to our schoolfellows at Dolgelley and our Master Daniel Evans and his family and to Griffith Thomas Maescaled and his family, and Owen Edward.

This briefly from your very loving
William G. Bebb.
[P.S.] Griffith be sure of writing to me too before long.

Van Wert County, Ohio
October 10, 1850
Mr. Griffith Owen
Vanner, Llanelltyd

Merioneth Shire, North Wales, Great Britain

Dear Brother,

I am able to inform you once again that we are all alive and well, as were our brother John and his family at Fort Winnebago, Wisconsin, the last time we heard from them — although they complained as we also might, that they never hear from you. We have not received one letter from you yet though we have sent two.

We have almost completed the building of our mills, one saw mill and one corn mill. There is only sufficient water for about a quarter of the year so we can expect few advantages but convenience. We had in past years and we have this year sown about twenty acres of wheat. We have about 120 acres of clear land, the remainder being woodland. As yet there are only twelve Welsh families here near us but others have bought land and will soon come, and there are others at a little distance from here.

We have about fifty persons amongst whom are 22 Methodist members, and practically all of us are abstainers, having recently renewed the pledge. The town of Pawnsydd about eight miles from here is growing very rapidly, both as regards size and trade; one may often see as many as a hundred wagons there in one day, selling wheat, etc. This will probably be a pleasant country before long, and although the Welsh come here but slowly, yet there is a large number of Englishmen. A farm, partly cleared, together with buildings, can be obtained for eight or twelve dollars per acre, and woodland from 2½ to 5 dollars per acre, but prices are rising near here.

The children have grown very much, William is powerfully built, Dafydd taller than I am, and Margaret almost as tall as Lowry, while Martha is fast following her; Jane is the smallest for her age, but she is quite healthy.

Last year was very dry so the crops were light, but with good ears [of corn] and the potato crop was good. We are still in much the same state as regards religious meetings, prayer meetings and school, etc. Two Methodist ministers have visited us, and Robert Williams Oak hill has promised to come soon. We lately received a letter from Richard Herbert of Montgomery promising to come here in the spring if we still continue to send for him and make the promises we made previously. We replied that we were prepared to do so, and that I would write to you without delay as before. The request I made in my last letter (if you received it) was that you would pay Richard Herbert £18, and Thomas Jones of Abergroes £2 (as well as the sum I paid for John) for his clothes. As the clothes were not fashionable I could not sell them for what they would pay, but they will now fit our boys and I hope to prevail upon them to wear them. Therefore I desire you to pay more, that is, £4 in all, to Thomas Jones, and £16 to Richard Herbert. If you pay readily in the manner I have directed I will not claim interest for the last three years, and their receipts will free you from my demand (and keep this as witness) until I send you the note. As you know it was May 13, 1846, that we last settled, and that you owe me £20, and that I owe you about ten shillings as I had not finished my payment for the children, and you chose to leave the 10s. 0d. towards the interest due the following year.

I request that you will write immediately to let me know that you have received this, and explain how every thing is to be done; we have not heard from you nor from Thomas Jones whether you received the £2 or not. Give me, too, a detailed account of yourself, and as much as possible of the news of neighbourhood and the best cause in the country. Your sister will be very pleased to receive news of her old home and her old friends.

Give our very loving regards to everyone who inquires about us, especially to the preachers and the church there and at Dolgelley. Do not delay in giving us much news from there; good news from a far country is like cool water to a thirsty man.

We unite to send you and your family and Owen and his family our kindest regards.

This from your brother and sister,

William and Margaret Bebb

P.S. R. Herbert means to start off for this country about the 25th of next March. If you have not the money ready now it would be a great encouragement to him and a convenience to me if you would write to tell him now that he will be certain to receive it by that time.

Edward Owen wrote the following letter to family members from a Louisiana house converted by the Union Army to field hospital, where he was convalescing, apparently from illness, not battle wounds. His report includes news about other Welsh soldiers, updates on the war's progress, and a declaration of unwavering faith despite his difficult circumstances.

Miliken's Bend, Louisiana
May 11th, 1863

Dear family at home,

There are many things I want to send to you but I do not know on what to start. I am now in a convalescent hospital; it is a house, through which a cannon bullet has passed. Before the regiment left it was its hospital, so it is quite comfortable compared with the majority of places. I have not been very well since William was here, and yet I have not been very ill either; I am sometimes better and sometimes worse. Many of us were left behind when the regiment went away, and we were to follow as soon as we were able, but our troops crossed the Miss. below Vicksburg in order to surround them from the back, so that those who were able to start after them were unable to cross the river to the regiment after all. We heard that they were fighting and that they were fairly victorious, but we do not believe all we hear now. Wm. Jones and H. Williams are here with me. Wm. Edwards was the only Welshman well enough to start with the company, and he looked strong and hearty when he started, Wm. Jones is rather thin now and continues to get diarrhoea, but Hugh is fat enough and very hearty; he is lame and suffers from backache. I do not quite know what is the matter with me; I suppose it is mostly the effect of the fever and occasional attacks of diarrhoea, although I have not been shivering since I am out. Perhaps that will be enough on that point.

I suppose you are very anxious to receive a letter from me by now. I delayed writing a long time, this time as I hoped to hear from Wm. after his return home, but as far as I know I am no nearer to hearing now. If you have not heard from me for a long while, I have been here a month and have received no letter from anywhere, although I have sent three I think. The mail bag is sent to the regiment, and the letters have to be sent to us from the Co., and as they are busy now, it is likely that no one but the Generals has mail now. They are fighting at Vicksburg these days; but I suppose you will have had a more detailed account of it than I can give you before you get this letter. In spite of that, I think that they are surrounding the place more skillfully this time than they did last time. They have gone to the country behind them, according to the report we hear, I do not know how much truth there is in that. We heard that they had destroyed the R.R. from Vick's[burg] to Jackson. The report states that it was done by cavalry, of whom there were but 1,500, who crossed the land through Miss. They destroyed 40 miles of road, 26 locomotives, a large number of cars, and a million rations. Of that, I believe that which you have certainty of its truth. As to my feelings I have little to say. I am not depressed because I am ill. I think that if I do not get better they will send the worst to the north when the battle is over. Do not worry too much on my account, it will not improve matters, my fate will be the same ever, and I believe that as strongly as I ever did. That which I can do now is to ask the Lord to cause me to know His ways, and lead me in his truth, and teach me here, in addition to taking pity on you there. I am glad to say that I feel a desire to breathe an occasional faint prayer on your behalf. Although I am so wretched and seek nothing, I am sometimes bet-

ter and sometimes worse, but the fact that I have the promise of the one
who cannot lie, to aid me, and that he will neither give me up nor completely leave me, is of comfort to me. On Sunday, a week yesterday, the
thought came to me anew that my love is like the rose of the field and the
lily of the valley; my love is fair, as the apple tree etc. In the midst of it all
I must give up, hoping this will reach you safely.

Let me know whether you received my wages from Madison, and my
great coat. Remember me to the boys and their families, as if I had mentioned them by name, and the neighbours in general, without exception.
Write to me as often as you can and accept my warmest regards.

I am yours,
Edward [Owen]

*T. Ll. Williams, who married one of John Owen's daughters and settled in
Racine, wrote this undated, unaddressed letter in response to a letter he had received giving news of family and friends in Wales.*

[Circa 1907]
I can do no less than express my thanks for your thoughtfulness in writing to me especially as you have so much other work to do. I thank you
also for the allusions to the persons with whom I came into contact there.
It is very strange to think that my cousin Annie Jones is no more, she
was always the guardian angel of the family in those parts. If any branch
of the family suffered illness or death, she always gave her valuable services. Mrs. Richards cannot but feel very sad at losing her; the two had
always been inseparable. I am pleased to think that Mr. Richards has
recovered. I am not at all surprised that you feel a great loss for your
kinswoman Miss Maggie Owen. She was very intelligent, and amiable,
and full of kindness; I found her especially so. I am pleased to think that
John Meyrick Jones is still so full of vitality. Be so good as to remember
me to him and to his amiable wife, and congratulate him on his pro-
motion to the magisterial bench in his native country. A cousin of his,
Mrs. John M. Roberts Brynglas, has come from their farm to live in this
city, she is sister to Mrs. Edwards of your town. If you are going on another journey to the East, I wish you good luck. But why not a journey to
the West first? Have you not been to the East once before? Everything is
so different on the continent of America from what it is on the continents

of Europe, Asia, and Africa. A visit to the United States is an education to people from this side. I follow movements there with detail as I get the "Goleuad" in exchange for the "Drych," from Griff Jones Davies, Greenfield, Holywell, and the "Cambrian News" from my nephew and namesake Thos. Lloyd Williams The Emporium, Rhos.

I trust that the House of Commons will not yield an inch to the House of Lords. "Trech Gwlad nac Arglwydd," (the country is stronger then its nobility) will be true again I hope. The governor of Jamaica played falsely did he not, with the American admiral who took there a supply of necessities to the needy, after the earthquake and the fire. I trust that the Government will discharge him unceremoniously as a lesson to him. [I] have almost finished reading the memoires of the Rev. Edwd Morgan. I seemed to live again the days of my youth as I read it, and it gives me a melancholy pleasure. The great work he accomplished with the disadvantage of having so frail a body is a marvel is it not. His melodious voice often echoes in my ears. There never has been and there is no one like him amongst the C.M. ministers. All the measures for which he debated so warmly and strongly have now been realised. We in Racine are engaged in building a new place of worship; it is almost finished. The cost will be over five thousand pounds, and over four thousand pounds have been promised. By the time the chapel is opened, the debt will have melted considerably, if not wholly wiped out. I was privileged to assist in building the old meeting house, fifty years ago, and it fell to my lot to collect towards the new meeting house as well. The generosity shewn amazes me. The Reverend John Davies has worked very strenuously to obtain the new place of worship. Note the state of affairs concerning it given in the next number of the "Drych." Will you and yours accept my kindest regards, and likewise Mr. And Mrs. Richards, Mr. And Mrs. Meyrick Jones, and also Richd and Evan Wynne Williams. They were all very kind to me. All Llew Meirion's relatives here are well. The Reverend John Davies has occasional bouts of illness. Mrs. Davies has acted like a lady and a Christian ever since she has been here. I see that the Reverend Gwynoro Davies is coming over here to visit us; a most suitable man to come. I understood that the Reverend Seth Joshua's ministry did not suit the congregations in this country; they were different from those to which he generally preaches there.

Affectionately,

T. Ll. Williams

In the following letter T. Ll. Williams refers to an enclosed letter written by a John Owen, whose lineage Williams provides. Unfortunately, the enclosed letter is not among the collection in the Wisconsin Historical Society Archives. Williams's letter nonetheless is of interest, especially in that he invites the recipients in Wales to a family reunion to be held in Caledonia, Wisconsin. The original letter had no paragraph breaks.

731 College Avenue,
Racine, Wisconsin.
March 11/[19]07
E.W. Evans, Esqre

Dear Friend,

I am pleased to be able to present you with the enclosed letter. Its author is the eldest son of Wm. Owen, the eldest son of Shion Owen, of Maesgarnedd, previously of 'Faner.' The letter explains itself. You will see that it would be advisable that John Owen's letter if not published should become the property of his grandson, John G. Owen of Portage, Wis.

J. G. O. has his father's relics, and indeed he is the only one of the family who is deeply interested in the past history of the family although his wife is American. He is as good a Welshman as regards language and feeling, as if he had been born and bred on the banks of the Mawddach or at the foot of Cader Idris.

The idea of holding a reunion, about the first of next July is an excellent one. Now I hope you will postpone your intended visit to the continent or Palestine, dear friend, until some later time, and take advantage of the family reunion meeting at Caledonia, Wisconsin, to be present there, especially as you intend visiting America sooner or later.

If, however, unavoidable obstacles prevent your visit, do not fail to act on the suggestion that you should send a letter there. It would be more profitable written in English, for although Shion Owen's children in their lifetime were unsurpassed as Welshmen, and for that matter his grandchildren, yet the greater number of his great-grandsons are better Englishmen, and they are now in the majority.

The one whose illness is mentioned is the son of the second John Owen, and his mother is my wife's sister.

A large number of Calvinistic Methodist ministers are coming over this year, and it is intended to open our new place of worship during the latter part of May; we have not decided on the exact date.

I send you and Mrs. Evans my sincerest regards and wish you to give my regards to Mr. and Mrs. Richards, the Bank, John M. Jones, and Richard Wynne Williams. I should like to have a reply from you, and hear your decision.

Yours truly,

T. Ll. Williams.

John Gwylyn Owen, mentioned in the letter above, wrote this letter from his home in Portage, Wisconsin, to Mr. Evans in Wales. He reflects on the Owen family's legacy, noting descendents, ". . . though not without faults they have some beautiful trails of character. . . ." The long, at times run-on sentences of the original, which were written in haste, were retained.

Portage June 10th, 1907

Dear Mr. Evans,

I received a letter from Mr. Thos. Ll. Williams Racine and within it was enclosed one from you[.] I showed it to the relatives here and we all feel very grateful for the interest you have taken pertaining to the history of our family[.] The letter was very interesting at this time and it established the date of their starting from Wales which helped to make the story of their emigration complete.

I am sending the notice we sent out in regard to the "Home Coming" and expect a large gathering on the fourth of July and so many of the family have expressed the wish that you could make us a visit in America and hope at some future day you can do so[.] Sorry to hear of the illness in your family and hope he will recover his health. We did think we would have to postpone the meeting here [as] the son of John Owen was very sick with stomach and heart trouble and did not know how things would turn, (hence [the] reason for the delay in writing and getting out the notice) but he is now on the gain and very enthusiastic over the homecoming.

The descendents of the Owen family are very numerous and though not without faults they have some beautiful traits of character which we can see now and appreciate such as Spirituality[.] Hospitality and the home and social ties were very marked. It was a great treat for them to get together and visit and it is plain to be seen that there must have been a strong desire in the family way back in Wales to keep little relics in remembrance of those who had gone before for it crops out here also.

We will have quite a display at the meeting among us all, several that came from Wales: I have grandfather's old bible; the "lly fr main" he had with Richard Mills and the one that father had later with temperance songs; a little shuttle father had made to make nets and fish with in W——, he gave it to Auntie Rice and she to me; he had saved letters from you and from Williams the pilot at Hong Kong, China; letters from Uncle Edward while in the army[.] I have them and a lot of things later which father had saved and are very valuable to me. Uncle Edward's letters show the true soldier spirit: "Achos ein glwad syd gengem a dyma yr unig ford I ni wasenethu yr srglwyd" oedd ei deoty d lyd yr oedd yr fackgen diniol fel ei fam yr hon oedd a digon a ras I medm gorfoleddn ae yr deodi ir Arglwyd am yr adgyfodiad ar lan y. Bedd pan yr daddu Edward ag Owen yu yr un bedd gydai gillid. [Translation of Welsh passage: The subject of his letters was continually that "Our cause is our country's cause, and that is the only way in which we can serve the Lord." He was a godly boy, and like his mother, who was so full of grace that she could rejoice and thank the Lord for the resurrection when standing beside the grave wherein Edward and Owen were buried together.]

I will write you a Welsh letter when I have more time and practice to spell. I am going to send you one of Uncle Edward's letters for you to keep as they are in Welsh. I will spare you this one out of the many he sent to them as it may be of interest to you and you can see from the tone of it his nature, the penmanship is not as good in this as he was sick.

There were one or two questions I wanted to ask you in regard to the pedigree that I don't fully understand[.] As near as I can make out from father's, Owen Pugh the father of David Owen, Vanen, and David father of John Owen, Maes — you also have Owen Pugh son of Hugh Owen, one letter. Aunt Rice told me David Owen was not the only child; your paper does not show any more than he. I expect you start at Jane Roberts on down [to the] wife of Owen Pugh without giving it in full. Aunt Lama used to say that they could trace the Owen family back 800 years. She got that impression when young. I have heard father and others tell it after Aunt Lama. What do you think about it? When did they come in possession of Vanen or the Abbey? Auntie Rice can remember sitting there in the place of Auntie Lama to get the tips the visitors gave for going through the old walls. A little early history in there would be very interesting to begin with. Of course we do not want to put it down unless it is so, and if it is true why not know it. We do not expect you to take any trouble at finding out these now unless you already know it but we would like to get a letter from you in time for this meeting[.] We can take those other matters up again.

I am writing this in a hurry in hopes that you will get it in time. Either english or welsh letter from Mr. Evans will be much appreciated and a copy of your paper would be a relic to keep. I will write you again more fully after the meeting. We expect Mr. Thos. Williams to be here at that time.

I must close and hoping you will get this in time to make a short letter any way.

Best regards to all from your family.

Yours truly

John Gwylyn Owen

East Cook St

Portage, Wisconsin

PRIVATE JOHN G. JONES LETTERS, 1862–1863

The following letters were written in 1862–1863 by John G. Jones to family members in Dodge County, Wisconsin, while he served in Company G, 23rd Wisconsin Infantry Regiment. The original spelling was retained.

Jones was one of many Welsh immigrants who volunteered to serve in the Union Army as most Welsh settlers were opposed to slavery and felt it their duty to fight against it and serve their new country.

Jones trained at Camp Randall in Madison and rose to the rank of Corporal. The 23rd Wisconsin saw action in the western theater of operations, mainly in Kentucky, Tennessee, Mississippi, Louisiana, and Texas. Jones's letters to his parents speak of his army experiences, but Jones also gives his thoughts about happenings on the homefront, lends advice to his younger brothers, and meditates on his faith. He sought out other Welsh soldiers and often mentions reading the Welsh newspaper Y Drych.

Corporal Jones died in a minor skirmish on October 5, 1864, in Sandy Bayou, Louisiana.

Camp Randol, Madison. August, Sunday, 31. 1862

My dear father and mother,

I hope that you are hearty as I am at present. We have been very busy drilling, and I had no time to write until today. I have had all my clothing today. We expect to receive our arms tomorrow. Some say that we will be going to Washington in two weeks. All the boys are well now. The boys like their uniforms pretty well. I have not been to the city after the first night. We have had our State Bounty yesterday, the bounty was 25. We were given this until we get our pay, we'll get that tomorrow, 15.

We expect our 100 dollars this week. I am trying to arrange a furlough for next week.

I am getting plenty of food. We expect to see somebody from our neighborhood coming to fetch our clothes. It is quite pleasant here, I have been talking to 18 Welshmen, strangers, six from Sawk County, three from Lake Cross, two from Praireducine [Prairie du Chien], seven from Spring Glen. We had to get up on Saturday to march to meet the twentieth regiment. You can imagine that they looked very fine as they marched past us. They numbered 1100, and the 23rd was all there, numbering about 1200 men all in their prime. I have been talking to the colonel and the major, they appear to be kindly men.

John G. Jones.

Memphis, Tenn. December 16. 1862.

Dear parents,

I take the occasion to address these few lines to you in the hope that they will find you as well as they leave me at present. I received your letter dated December 1st, and I was very glad of it. I do not know where all the letters you write go to, they must go somewhere. I sent a note in Thomas Hughes's letter asking you to send me some money. We were disappointed in not receiving our pay, I have been without any money for about two weeks. I would like to have some money, they tell us that we are sure to get our pay at the end of this month if I am alive by then. I am enjoying better health than ever, the weather is something like June, but it is quite cold at night. I think that this climate agrees with me better than Wisconsin. I enjoy a soldier's life very much, but I did not enjoy being on the water as much as being on land. I had heard that we were to go towards Vicksburg within a few days, but I do not think it is true. We stand picket duty once every ten days, and camp guard once every six days.

I would like to know who is keeping school in the school house this winter. I would also like to know how things are our way regarding drafting for the army, and other things also. I have heard that the 28 Wis Vol. have been fighting the mobs. I have seen some of the draftees who have been sent to make up the numbers in the old regiments. I would not like to see any of the Welsh boys from around Salem being sent to do that. If any of them are drafted it would be better for them to escape and enlist if they can.

Well, I must conclude by wishing you all success spiritually and materially. I am in strong hope that I may be allowed to come home before very long. It is nearly four months since we are bearing arms. Time passes quickly. I would like to know which of John McMalan's daughters died. All the boys are well and wish to be remembered to you kindly. We have not heard from Fred yet.

John G. Jones. Co. G. 23 Wis. Vol.

Memphis, Tenn.

First regiment, first brigade, first division.

Millikens Bend Encampment, La. Tuesday, March 30. 1863.
Dear Parents,

I take advantage of this opportunity to send you a few lines in the hopes that they will find you alive and well, the same as they leave me at present. God be thanked for keeping us in the land of the living, and within the bounds of hope. I do not have much news today, I hoped to have had a letter when the mail came in yesterday. I decided to write today after hearing that Richard is well again, I was very glad that he is better. You have probably heard that John Owanes, and Owan Owanes, and John Jones the tailor are sick in the hospital. O. O. and John O. are getting better. Rob Williams and Evan Richard have been very ill. Thos. Hughes, John W. Jones, Rees Cook, Jonah and myself are standing the climate first rate so far. I heard yesterday that our division is to go up the river to Kentucky. I hope that the rumor is true. There are so many stories about this and about that, that it is impossible to know what to believe. The 11 Wis. came here last week from Pilot Knob, Mo. The 11 Regt. Wis. is between Cairo and Vicksburg. We expect an attack on Vicksburg every day. We have found Welsh boys in the 22 Iowa and the 25 Iowa and the 108 Illinois, there seems to be very many Welsh boys in the army.

We hear that there is a great deal of commotion in the Old State of Wisconsin over the draft. A word to Richard and Owen, my brothers: you are both too young for the draft, do not enlist while you can stay home. Do as I tell you, do not do as I did. Although I do not regret coming. I have a strong feeling that I shall come home again, but when I do not know. Our living conditions are excellent since we settled here, plenty to eat and to wear so as to keep us trim, we drill twice a day, and then we exercise ourselves, so as to keep idleness away.

Our Orderly Sergeant has been promoted 2 Lieutenant, the old 2nd. is still here. The old Captain has not been given command of the Company yet, and I hope that there will be no change. I must close now. From
     John G. Jones.

Vicksburg Camp, Miss. July 27, 1863
Beloved Parents and Brothers,
I take this opportunity to write these few lines hoping that they will find you enjoying your usual health, as I am at present through the

great goodness and mercy of the Lord towards us who are so wicked.

I received your kind letter dated July 20 today, and the one dated July 13, also *Y Drych*. I was very glad of them having been without mail for so long. I was amazed to hear that you had cut the back field in such a short time. You enquire how I hurt my finger. The doctor said that it was cut by a piece of shell which burst right over my head, it is well again by now. The mail comes in quite regularly since Vicksburg fell. I cannot tell you anything you cannot read in the newspapers. The people had holes in the ground where they hid when the shelling was on.

I have not had a single letter from R. H. Jones; I wrote to him a fortnight ago, and I am expecting an answer. Owen Owens, Co. G, has had his discharge, and Hugh T. Williams has gone on a 60 day furlough. They are starting to give the boys furloughs today, the married men go first.

I do not know when I shall get home, I shall try when the next opportunity comes along in a month or six weeks. We have just had the heaviest thunder-shower I ever saw, the wind wrecked our tents. T. E. Hughes and John W. Jones are well and wish to be most kindly remembered to you. T. E. Hughes wrote home today.

There is a great deal of traffic on the Miss. from Cairo to New Orleans. We are camping on the river side, and it is good to see the water of the Mississippi once again. They are arranging for us to remain here for some time, at least over another pay day, they say we shall go up the river afterwards, fit for duty once again. I am in good health and feeling fine. You were saying that you thought I would have learnt English by now. I now prefer to speak English to Welsh, it is easier as we are continually with the English. Willie Roberts and his brother Hugh Roberts from Co. E 23rd are clever lads. W. Edwards Co. C is rather wild, the only one of the 6 or so.

Night is catching up with me, so I must conclude and take my letter to the P.O. I wish to be remembered to you most kindly, wishing you every material and spiritual blessing. I hear that John T. Edwards is going to enlist again, I would advise him to stay home. I should think he has suffered enough without attaching himself again. I wish to be remembered lovingly to all.

Lovingly yours,

John G. Jones.

[P.S.] The bands sound the reveille every morning, and the tatoo at night. They are much pleasanter to hear than the guns.

Camp near New Iberia, La. Nov 25th./63.

Respected Parents and Brothers,

~~The Mercy and Graciousness together with the care of the good Lord~~ allow me to greet you once again while amongst the living, and within the bounds of hope. I hope that these lines will find you all enjoying health and happiness, as they leave me. I received your kind letter last night, and also the piece from J. T. Williams. I was glad to see the old Pilgrim's handwriting. Remember me to him in the most kindly way, and tell him that I hope to see his handwriting again soon. I am exceedingly glad to hear that you are succeeding so outstandingly in worldly matters, and I hope that spiritual matters are also prospering in the neighborhood of Salem. I have heard that the Lord's work is at a low ebb in Salem. I am sorry to hear that the boys are so wild and uncivilized in that area. I heard that one or two of them have been censured by the Society. They should be ashamed to be so wicked in such a favoured place. I have seen the mistakes I made when I was within reach of better things; I refused advice and many things which would have helped me. I heard that some of the boys caused a fuss around Columbus recently, and that they have been reprimanded by members of the Society.

We are still without a Chaplain in the Regt., there are preachers in the other regiments. There are several colored regiments here, and they have colored preachers. They preach excellent sermons, and they attract the boys more than our own preachers. They have a great talent. I like the colored troops just as well as the white ones. J. W. Jones has returned to me again healthy and wishes to be remembered to you one and all most kindly. Everything is going on very well down here now. The 3rd Corps recently took over a hundred rebs, including 12 of their officers. I think the rebs have retreated to somewhere near the Red River, I heard yesterday that they were firing with cannons at our boats by the mouth of the Red River a week ago yesterday. Three of the shells hit the boat, one exploded in the pilot house, no one on board was hurt, it was a foggy morning. I was amazed to know the amount of wheat you had, and I was glad to hear that Owan is getting better. I heard that the people around there feared the draft, I would like to see some of them coming down here. I have no more news at present. There is a rumor that the Orderly Sergeant is going home to recruit men to fill our thinning ranks. It is difficult to believe all we hear. I heard that our Brigade is to go to Memphis to be made up to strength. General Burbridge is doing his best to have the brigade sent up the river. I must end this short and untidy letter from

J. G. Jones.

[P.S.]I wish to be remembered to you one and all in the most kindly way, and to J. T. Williams as well as to Owan Morris. I received a letter from Owan Morris two days ago.

SELECTED BIBLIOGRAPHY
AND FOR FURTHER READING

Berthoff, Rowland Tappan. *British Immigrants in Industrial America, 1790–1950*. (Cambridge: Harvard University Press, 1953; 2nd ed., New York: Russell and Russell, 1968.)

Chidlaw, B. W. "The American: Which Contains Notes of a Journey from the Ohio Valley to Wales." Translated by Rev. M. O. Evans. *Quarterly Publication of the Historical and Philosophical Society of Ohio*, VI: 1–41 (January 1911). [Originally published in 1840.]

Conway, Alan, editor. *The Welsh in America: Letters from the Immigrants*. (Minneapolis: University of Minnesota Press, 1961.)

Davies, Rev. Howell D., translator. *Oshkosh, Wisconsin, Welsh Settlement Centennial, 1847–1947*. (Amarillo, Texas: Russell Stationery Co., 1947.)

Hartmann, Edward George. *Americans from Wales*. (Boston: Christopher Publishing House, 1967; 2nd ed., New York: Octagon Books, 1978.)

Knebel, Melva. *In the Shadows of the Mines: The Village of Rewey, Wisconsin, 1880–1980*. (Dodgeville, Wisconsin: Dodgeville Chronicle, 1980.)

Thomas, Rev. Robert D. "The Welsh in Wisconsin: Thomas Hanes Cymry America." Translated by Phillips G. Davies. *The Old Northwest*, V: 269–289 (Fall 1979.)

Williams, Daniel Jenkins. *One Hundred Years of Welsh Calvinistic Methodism in America*. (Philadelphia: Westminster Press, 1937.)

Williams, Daniel Jenkins. *The Welsh Community of Waukesha County*. (Columbus, Ohio: Hann and Adair, 1926.)

INDEX

Page numbers referencing photos or illustrations are in italic type.

THE AUTHOR

PHILLIPS G. DAVIES, a third-generation Welsh-American, graduated from Marquette University in 1946 and earned advanced degrees from Northwestern University. He was a longtime professor of English at Iowa State University in Ames, Iowa. His publications include studies of Thackeray, Shelley, and Hemingway, and translations of accounts about Welsh settlements, mostly in the Midwest.